MW01504006

OUT, OUT, BRIEF CANDLE!

Out, Out, Brief Candle!

Macbeth Comes to
Africa's Children of Fire

Martin Klammer

WIPF & STOCK · Eugene, Oregon

Wipf & Stock
An Imprint of Wipf and Stock Publishers
199 W. 8th Ave., Suite 3
Eugene, OR 97401

www.wipfandstock.com

PAPERBACK ISBN: 978-1-5326-4787-1
HARDCOVER ISBN: 978-1-5326-4788-8
EBOOK ISBN: 978-1-5326-4789-5

JULY 30, 2018

To the children of fire
for their great love and courage

"God didn't mean that if you are burned people mustn't love you. We have to love one another, because he created us the same. We are the same. We have the same souls—it doesn't matter just because we are burned as children of fire."

NTHABISENG NKASHE

Contents

CONTENTS

Introduction

THIS SMALL BOOK IS a record of my time with Children of Fire, a non-profit organization in Johannesburg, South Africa that provides rehabilitation for child survivors of serious burns throughout the African continent, mostly from southern Africa. Children of Fire is the only full-time care center for child burn survivors in Africa. The center houses between six and forty children undergoing surgery, occupational therapy, and physiotherapy. To date, Children of Fire has helped 450 child burn survivors.

Please note: in the text Children of Fire (capitalized) refers to the charity; children of fire (lower case) refers to the children themselves as a group.

In quoting from the writings of the children, I have not altered their spelling or grammar—not to point out deficiencies, but to capture the authenticity of their writing voices.

All proceeds from this book will be donated to Children of Fire.

1

February 2: "They Shall be Comforted"

SOUTH AFRICA IS A kind of second home to me. I am a professor of English at Luther College in Decorah, Iowa, USA, who has come to South Africa almost every year for twenty years, sometimes with students, sometimes with family, and now by myself for a sabbatical in Johannesburg. I am staying at a lovely little bed and breakfast in Auckland Park, a suburb a few miles west of the city center.

This morning I decided to attend St. Peter's Anglican Church, just across the street. Shortly after I sat down, six young women crowded into my pew before the service started. Not really seeing them at first, I moved to my right to make room.

Then I looked up.

The face of the girl next to me was wholly burn-scarred, like a darker mask over her black skin with two eyes peering out. I tried not to look shocked, but I suppose I did. The girl next to her had a burn mark from her neck through her shoulder into the arm and hand. The girl next to her was on crutches; when she went up to communion I saw she had only one leg. Younger children also came to communion from Sunday school. Most were visibly burned, two of them so badly burned that parts of their ears and noses were missing. And yet all of these children seemed happy, not troubled by their appearance. The girl next to me even became my pew buddy as she showed me when to use one of the three hymnals, the service book, or the "pew leaflet" (bulletin). At the end of the service she even shared her hymnal with me.

Reverend Williams, a tall, regal-looking mixed-race woman, preached on the Beatitudes from the Sermon on the Mount in which Jesus says:

> *Blessed are the poor in spirit, for theirs is the kingdom of heaven.*
> *Blessed are those who mourn, for they shall be comforted.*
> *Blessed are the meek, for they shall inherit the earth.*
> (Matt 5:3-5, RSV)

Her sermon focused on how the Beatitudes are about community. When those who mourn shall be comforted, she said, the comfort doesn't descend from the heavens in the form of an angel or a bolt of lightning. It comes from us. We are the comforters.

After the service, visitors were asked to introduce themselves. I went first. When Reverend Williams heard I was from the United States, she joked (a bit pointedly I thought), "Sorry, you can't join us. You can't afford to." Then one of the six girls in my row—not disabled, as far as I could see—said she was "also" from the children's center, so I assumed they came from a group home.

I had to find out where these children came from, so after lunch I googled combinations of words like "burn," "victim," "children," and "Johannesburg." Up popped Children of Fire, a charitable organization that treats and is home to child burn survivors throughout Africa. I checked my map: it was just three blocks away! I knew I had to visit. I wanted to know if this was an organization where I could take my American students for a service-learning experience. More than that, I wanted to know how burned children could be so happy.

February 3: "Out, Out, Brief Candle!"

AT THE CHILDREN OF Fire office on a leafy street in Auckland Park, I was met at the gate by a young female volunteer from Belgium who ushered me past a swimming pool and yard on the left into a corridor of offices. Several young women, black and white, looked up from their computer screens and smiled. The volunteer and I went through to a cluttered back office where the she left me in the hands of Bronwen Jones, the organization's director.

Bronwen is my age—mid-fifties—tall, with long auburn hair and a cherubic ruddy face. She was in the middle of several things—giving directions to a volunteer, responding to an email, answering the phone. After inviting me to sit on a back-less broken chair, she thrust a volunteer application form into my hands on her way out to speak briefly with the volunteers.

"I'm not here for this," I said as she brushed past me.

When she returned I explained that I was on sabbatical as a visiting scholar at the University of the Witwatersrand (known as Wits). I told her how struck I was by the six girls in church and the smaller children who came forward for communion. "They all seemed so happy," I remarked. I said I hoped that in my January course to South Africa her organization might provide a good service opportunity for my students, if we could do something useful without getting in the way. "But I'm not here to volunteer," I repeated.

"You will be," she said.

"I'm a professor of literature," I protested. "What could I possibly do?"

She reached into a stack of papers and books on her desk and pulled out a copy of *Macbeth*.

"Teach this," she said.

"Seriously?"

"Seriously."

She had my interest. I had in fact thought I might like to do volunteer work in South Africa, but this came upon me so suddenly I didn't know how to respond. I asked how old the children were. She said around fourteen and fifteen. That seemed doable. I had read *Macbeth* as a fifteen-year-old in high school, and a friend back in Iowa directs children that age in performances of Shakespeare that are genuinely good. Still, I didn't know the ability of these kids at Children of Fire and whether I really wanted to jump in feet-first after having been in the office less than five minutes, so I changed the subject. I asked Bronwen her story, and how she had got there. She deferred, saying simply that she was a British woman who had come to South Africa more than twenty years ago with her husband and young son. She had found out about an infant girl in hospital who was so badly burned the doctors were going to let her die, but Bronwen wasn't going to let that happen. I could read about it on the website, she said, a refrain I would hear many times in the coming weeks.

As Bronwen talked, I looked around the office. The walls were festooned with graphic before-and-after surgery pictures of young black children that were sometimes hard to look at: hands, faces, and skulls that had been horribly burned and that even in repair were not pretty. I pointed to a picture of a teenage girl with what I thought was a creative ornament on the side of her head. Bronwen explained that that was the girl's skin, inflated with a liquid that created a balloon of flesh which was then moved, cut, and molded into place to provide hair for the girl. It was a common surgery, Bronwen said, one the children undergo all the time.

"One or more of our children are often in head bandages from these surgeries," she said. "You'll see that when you work with them."

It was then that I offered to start mentoring the children on *Macbeth*.

"When do I start?" I asked.

"Why not tomorrow?" she replied.

3

February 5: "Upon the Health"

WHEN I ARRIVED AT Bronwen's office today, I told her I had a couple of questions before I got started. She said "Take the hot seat," spinning a chair so that I could sit down.

"Why did you choose *Macbeth*," I asked her, "or any Shakespeare for that matter, rather than something else?"

"Someone sent me the book," she said, "but it wasn't just because I had the book. I love the play and I love Shakespeare. These kids will have to learn Shakespeare as one of their set pieces in high school. This will prepare them for that. Who knows? They may even get to like it."

She smiled.

"Maybe it has something to do with the fact that when I was a teenager I had a boyfriend named Banquo. But mostly it's because I know these kids can do anything. We get them to aim high: Kilimanjaro and then the stars."

Kilimanjaro wasn't a metaphor, she went on to tell me. Seventeen youth from Children of Fire had climbed Kilimanjaro and Bronwen was planning to take others to climb Ethiopia's highest peak.

We agreed I could teach anything I wanted, but I said I would stick with *Macbeth*. She then thought out loud about my acting troop, sounding like a mother hen assessing each of her brood: "She's a bit slow as a reader but maybe this will inspire her." "She'll be great if you can just get her to sit still." "I don't know what's up with him lately but maybe this is the chance he needs." These were her kids, albeit far more than any parent would have, along with the complication that, when I asked how long they stayed, she said, "Two days, two months, two years, twenty years." And one more complication in her life and now mine: on any given day one or more of the children would be in hospital. This day four were to have had surgery but two surgeries had been postponed.

Bronwen asked a female volunteer from the University of Johannesburg to walk me the few blocks to the school, called The Johannesburg School for the Blind, Low Vision and Multiple Disability Children. Bronwen started the school when she felt the public schools could not—or would not—educate one of the burn children who was blind. So the burn children and blind children learn together, with the children of fire practicing braille along with their visually handicapped classmates.

The school grounds are fairly small, with a small courtyard and an L-shaped building around the playground like a peninsula. I was taken to a classroom outfitted with a small table and three chairs, with a fourth broken chair shoved off to the side. A couple of smaller children wandered in while I set up, but they were soon seized and pulled back by unseen hands of older kids admonishing them in Zulu or Sotho.

One by one my students walked in. As I pulled the table to make room for the girl with one leg, it shifted off its foundation and slid toward the floor. The girl quickly put a brick back in place that had been supporting the table.

"It's all right, sir," she said, meaning, I think, that not only was it okay that I had knocked the table off its foundation but also that she didn't need any help. And indeed she didn't, as the afternoon was to prove.

I asked the children to introduce themselves. As they spoke, I wrote down their names, ages, and home areas in a school exercise book Bronwen had given me.

Lance Van Rooyen, age eleven, is a mixed-race boy from "west of Jo'burg" he said. He wears thick glasses and is a bit thick set. He is a day learner—not burned, but visually disabled.

Nthabiseng Nkashe, seventeen, is from Lichtenburg in the North West province. She is the amputee, tall and thin, and speaking quickly with a kind of nervous energy.

Dikeledi Mboko, eleven, is from Lesotho. She looks older, perhaps fourteen, and speaks quietly.

Anele Nyongwana, thirteen, from Mthatha in the Eastern Cape, is the girl with the facial burns who sat next to me at church.

I thought I would be working with children ages fourteen to fifteen, so having three kids younger than that threw me for a loop. I introduced myself by writing my name in large letters on a piece of paper: *Professor Martin Klammer*. Then I drew a crude map of Europe and Africa on the right side and North and South America on the left, making a little star where Iowa was and telling them that was where I was from and it was minus-twenty degrees celsius there. That didn't seem to register much, so we got down to business.

I figured I had better start with the basics so I asked them if they had heard of Shakespeare. No, they hadn't. I told them he was a famous writer from England who lived 400 years ago. I had four used copies of *Macbeth* that I had bought the previous day at Wits and when I held one up to show them they reached for the other three, Nthabiseng grabbing first. I told them *Macbeth* was a story of someone who wanted to be a king and asked if they knew what a king was.

"He is a ruler!" Nthabiseng said.

"Yes," I said. "And how does a person get to be king?"

"He must just be nice to his people," Anele said.

"Yes, that's what he's *supposed* to do," I said. "But does anyone know how he gets to be a king?" They didn't, so I explained how the eldest son of the king gets to be the next king, and I compared that to an African chief, which they understood.

"Is there another way one might become a king?" I asked. They didn't know, so I said dramatically, "He *kills* the king and takes over." Surprisingly, that also didn't register much, but when I said the play *Macbeth* started with three witches, *that* piqued their interest.

The first thing we had to do was *find* where the play began in their books after all the introductory material. After looking at the cast of characters we turned to the opening scene and I assigned parts: Witch 1-Lance; Witch 2-Dikeledi; Witch 3-Nthabiseng. Anele and I would be the sounds of thunder and lightning that open the play.

When I asked Lance to start reading, his head was bent down so close to the text I thought he had fallen asleep. But then I saw that he had to be that close just to *see* the words—his nose almost touching the page, his head moving across as he pronounced each word. Even with this challenge, he was a good reader.

Dikeledi was also a good reader, but when she made errors Nthabiseng immediately corrected her, growing increasingly frustrated each time Dikeledi said the witches would next meet "Upon the *health*." Nthabiseng, for her part, proved a quick study, and intuitively dramatic. They read:

Lance: "Where the place?"

Dikeledi: "Upon the health."

Nthabiseng: "*Heath!* There to meet with [pause] Macbeth!"

All three then joined in the eerie rhythm of "Fair is foul and foul is fair/Hover through the fog and filthy air."

When they got their lines down I stressed that these were witches they were playing, old hags, so could they come up with a good witchy voice? I performed my high-pitched craggy witch voice and they cheerfully sounded off theirs. Lance's was squeaky, Nthabiseng's a low growl. Then we went outside to practice in the driveway, as if onstage, while several little kids from the school looked through the bars of a locked gate. I told my actors that this scene was often performed with a huge cauldron that the witches stirred. Nthabiseng lifted her crutch, stood on her one leg, and with the crutch stirred an imaginary pot. Some of the little kids laughed, but I could see they were impressed.

When the three witches performed the scene I saw that we had a new problem: they were *too* witchy—so witchy in fact I couldn't tell what they were saying. I reminded them that they needed to be understood. They then performed the scene beautifully to cheers and applause from the little ones, and we walked back inside.

Bronwen had told me that an hour of rehearsal would be enough. We'd been at it for more than an hour, but the children wouldn't let me go. Lance said his ride wouldn't arrive for another twenty minutes. Okay, I said. But I was wary of the complexity in the next scene in which a wounded captain reports to King Duncan in a series of metaphors about Macbeth's war heroics. I read the speech as dramatically and clearly as I could, then did my best to explain what it meant.

One thing I explained was Fortune, smiling at first on Macbeth's enemy Macdonwald. I drew a rough picture of Lady Fortune on the Wheel of Fortune, and showed how, as the wheel turned, one's fortunes went up or down. I placed each of the four students on the wheel for the sake of example, putting Anele on her way down.

"This is you, Anele, falling from good fortune to bad fortune."

"No!" she said, startled.

Nthabiseng laughed and explained that this was just an example. And yet the image did get me to think about *their* fortunes. These kids had been terribly burned (except for Lance). Were their fortunes on the way up? Would they ever be?

Since Nthabiseng was often finishing others' lines (even when I asked her not to), it was clear I had to give her a challenge, so I asked her to read the captain's speech. She made her way slowly at first, but on the second try she executed it so well that when she finished Anele exclaimed breathlessly "Oh, my!" and the others burst into applause.

When we ended the class, the children broke into a "Thank you" song led by Nthabiseng, one I would hear many times for myself or others, and always led by Nthabiseng.

Signing the guest book in the main building on my way out, I was surrounded by kids of all ages just being kids, yelling and shouting and shoving in that manic energy that comes to children before dinner. One of the younger girls was particularly scarred, her skull completely burnt into a layer of seared skin. But this didn't stop Lance from sitting on top of her on a chair until she protested and others pulled him off. They seemed to be part of one big family.

As I left the school I heard Nthabiseng shout behind me: "When shall we three meet again?"

4

February 10: "That's a Nose"

TODAY WE HAD FIVE "actors"—Lance, Nthabiseng, and Anele, plus two new actors, Feleng and Wendy.

Feleng is the facially and head-scarred young man whose appearance first struck me when the younger children walked up to communion in church. He is missing part of his nose and eyebrows, and much of his skull is hairless. But he's such a character that after a while you don't see him as different but as a kid with a wandering attention span and quirky personality. Before we got started Feleng was asked by a teacher to take a younger blind boy out to the school bus. He grabbed the poor kid by the wrist and dragged him over. It was quite a sight: the physically disfigured Feleng hauling the blind boy, his head looking skyward as if to pray that Feleng wouldn't push him onto the pavement.

Wendy, the other newbie, is an eighteen-year-old volunteer and recent high school graduate hoping to get into a university to study mechanical engineering. She is short and slight, her beauty enhanced by a quiet grace. She was the young woman who first spoke up in church. She seemed to enjoy reading *Macbeth* with us, playing Banquo to Nthabiseng's Macbeth.

The witches—now Lance, Feleng, and Anele—started getting into their roles. Feleng even came up with a scary Halloween witch's voice (*nay-ah-hah-hah-heeeee!*) to conclude just about every line he spoke. And their chant of "Fair is foul and foul is fair" was a sight to behold, their heads bobbing up and down as they circled the cauldron in sing-song unison. Howling in demonic laughter and screeching "when the hurly-burly is done," these disfigured or nearly-blind kids looked, well, witchy!

After we finished and I went to sign out, I peeked into the kitchen to see why the children were making so much noise. I shuddered. Unsupervised, they were stirring a large pot of soup, pretending to be witches over the boiling cauldron. They chanted and stirred so vigorously it looked as if they would pull the pot over and scald themselves.

"Careful!" I said.

Then I turned and noticed what looked like a piece of chocolate on the counter.

"What's this?" I asked Feleng.

He turned it over. "Oh that," he said. "That's a nose."

<h2 style="text-align:center">5</h2>

February 11: "Happy as Larry"

SOMEONE IN THE DIVERSITY Studies office at Wits, where I occasionally go to check in and bother the staff, reminded me that I was the Writing Director at my college and wondered if I might want to have the children do some writing. Oh yes, I thought, that's not a bad idea!

So today I gave each child an individualized writing notebook with different covers (the earth, a flower, a zebra, cartoon characters) that I bought at Pick-n-Pay. (Nthabiseng chose first, taking the cover of Barbie in capri pants.) I asked them to write their name and address on the inside cover. I didn't expect them to write out "Johannesburg School for the Blind, Low Vision and Multiple Disability Children," and they didn't. Instead they wrote "Beka."

"What's Beka?" I asked.

"It's the name of our school," someone said. "It means 'look.'"

Almost two weeks with them and I didn't know! Bronwen later gave me a school brochure. Lance is on the cover, pointing to a word about six inches away. At the top in a child-like script is the word "Beka." Below is the school symbol: an eye with the continent of Africa in place of the pupil.

For their first writing I gave them the easiest, most inviting prompt I could think of: "Tell us about a happy day in your life."

They seemed surprised, even startled, to be asked to "just write" and had a hard time getting started; after fifteen minutes of their inactivity and my cajoling, I almost called it off.

Munashe asked what would come to be her trademark for our writing sessions: a question with the answer embedded.

"We are to write about a happy day, neh?"

"Yes, just tell us about a happy day. But do it in writing."

"What are we to write about?"

I was starting to lose patience and so were a couple others who said "Munashe!" But then Nthabiseng stepped in with more authority than I could muster.

"You are to write about a happy day," Nthabiseng said. "Just write down what you remember from a happy day."

That seemed to do the trick. Munashe started writing. In fairness to her, as Bronwen later pointed out, Munashe only learned English when she came to Children of Fire two years ago as a twelve-year-old orphan along with her cousin Clara, ten, both badly injured in a shack fire in Zimbabwe.

Lance finished first, after about five minutes and thirty words.

"Don't you have more to say?" I asked.

He looked closely at his writing, picked up his pencil and wrote another sentence. The others wrote little more. They just took longer. Nthabiseng was the most fluent, as she is orally. But it was Anele who offered to read first.

> *My birthday was on 15 March on Friday at the morning I went to hospital with Munashe at barha it was also Clara's birthday so Clara and I we sheareing a same date. The was another lady who came to fach us a four in the morning she brought us cake and prezens we had our stuff after we dance and dance. So doctor zeen said Happy birthday Clara because he didn't know that it was my birthday too. When we came back, we went to magdonald to eat our breakfast. When we were back home I find cake's ful of fregh I was so so happy lik never before The END.*

Anele's reading out loud was easier to follow than her writing. Her errors may have been the result of quick writing without proofreading ("The" for "There"), but they also suggested a young person whose learning had been disrupted by multiple surgeries and extended hospital time.

Bronwen later explained Anele's essay to me. Anele and Clara, Munashe's younger cousin, share a March 15 birthday. The previous year, Clara had charmed a woman who had had plastic surgery on her ward at Chris Hani-Baragwanath Hospital in Soweto ("*bar-ha*") into treating her on her birthday. The woman fetched ("*fach*") Anele and Munashe (at 6:00 am, Bronwen thinks, not 4:00) to take them to see Clara at the hospital. Bronwen, opposed to strangers giving things to the children, agreed to this as long as Anele was included. Bronwen called the woman an "ag-shamer," one of those people, she wrote in an email, "who have a synthetic candyfloss useless type of pity where they often do more harm than good, and where they judge Children of Fire and me on their standards for 'those poor children' and want to give them things or do things with them that they would not dream of doing for or with their own children."

(I was to see this behavior all too often: school groups or families bringing "gifts" without consulting Bronwen and staying just long enough to get a photo, often posing with the children of fire, whom they had seen only once or twice before, or not at all. One Afrikaner woman came by with her chubby son and dropped off boxes of chips and cool drink [pop]. She, too, got a photo of herself with the children which she was going to post on Facebook as part of a charity competition.)

For the happy day writing, three of the children chose the same day when they took a trip to Durban on the Indian Ocean. Nthabiseng and Lance each wrote that the day "was hot as hell" and they were "happy as Larry." Nthabiseng wrote she was excited to see "ostrich, impala. Those are the animals that I never seen them in my life." But the real fun for her was simply being on a road trip with the others: "I was sitting at the back seat with Lance, Nhlanhla, Munashe, Khanyisile, and Nelson. We ate and Nhlanhla told us, 'Eat, drink and be merry for tomorrow we will die.'"

Portrait: Anele Nyongwana

Every child here has a story, often one of terrible pain and of resilience. During my term at Children of Fire, I heard many of their stories from Bronwen.

Anele Nyongwana, who I sat next to that first Sunday, came to Children of Fire in February 2006, just before she turned six. She had been living with her family in Eikenhoff, a black settlement an hour from Johannesburg. When Anele was three months old a candle fell over, setting fire to the paper covering the walls of the shack that was her family home. Anele's face and hands were badly burned. Bronwen says that, according to Anele's family, when she was admitted to Baragwanath the nurses informed her father, Moses, that she wouldn't make it and they suggested she be given an injection to let her "slip away." Moses refused and requested to speak to the doctors. He stayed with his daughter that night. In the end, she survived.

Early on, Anele struggled not only physically but emotionally. She was so afraid of what other burn survivors looked like that when she saw Feleng and two other boys playing on the school grounds she ran into the street in fear. But with the kindness of the other children, Bronwen's attention, and the passage of time, Anele adjusted and is happy today.

Like many children of fire, Anele underwent tissue expansion surgery to restore her hairline. Tissue expansion enables the body to "grow" extra skin to help reconstruct almost any part of the body. In the United States and other Western countries, tissue expansion is most commonly used to create a false breast after a mastectomy, but it's also used to repair skin damaged by birth defects, surgery, and accidents such as burns. In tissue expansion surgery, a silicone balloon is inserted under the skin which is then filled through a valve with saline, making the skin stretch and grow. The incision is sutured, leaving just enough of an opening for further saline injections. After the incision is healed, the patient is given additional injections periodically to enlarge the tissue expander and further stretch the skin. When enough skin has expanded to cover the defect, a second surgery is performed to remove the expander. The new tissue is repositioned over the area needing repair and sutured in place, completing the reconstruction.[1]

Anele Nyongwana

For children with burns, tissue expansion is most often used to create hair in places burned so deeply that hair roots have been lost. Tissue expanders are inflated beneath the remaining good hair which is then stretched and eventually cut and stitched into place so that skin with hair roots covers the whole scalp. The procedure does not produce more hair, but redistributes the same amount of hair over a wider area. Bronwen described it as a bit like the difference between a lush lawn and scrubland. She added: "It's like being pregnant on your head. When it stretches the skin exactly how you want it, you cut and move the skin over and the child looks almost normal. Then they feel happy."

As beneficial as the process can be, it can also be painful or risky. If the burn injury has left little hair, tissue expansion may not be worth the cost and discomfort. The face or scalp may require multiple procedures, any one of which risks infection, excessive bleeding, poor wound healing, persistent pain, and leaking or even breaking of the tissue expander. The child may also be subject to ridicule from other children who think she looks funny with a

1. American Society of Plastic Surgeons, "Tissue Expansion," paras. 1–2, 12–14.

bulge the size of a cricket ball on her head.[2] At Children of Fire, the children are not ridiculed because almost every one of them will have had a tissue expander.

In Anele's case, when she came to Children of Fire her facial skin was so contracted from scar tissue that she could not close her eyes and mouth while sleeping. The following year at age seven, Anele was operated on at Sunninghill Hospital, a private health care facility in the wealthy suburb of Sandton, known to have excellent pediatric specialists. Dr. Martin Kelly successfully loosened and relaxed the skin on Anele's face.

While I was at Children of Fire, I found Anele to be a hard worker, always attentive to what I asked and impatient with others when they were not. Anele is also very kind, as she showed when she helped me negotiate the hymn and prayer books at church. She likes and wants to be responsible, such as holding and rocking the baby boy Rien, a six-month-old from the Congo with serious facial and head burns. Like the other girls, Anele enjoys singing and dancing. When the music is playing, she really likes to shake it!

---

2. "Tissue Expanders," paras. 16–21.

6

February 18: "Granny Didn't Hear the Fire"

TODAY THE CHILDREN WROTE about a sad day. At the end of our writing about a happy day Lance had said, "Next time we must write about a *sad* day." I didn't know what this would elicit from the kids and I didn't want to pry into their pain as burn survivors. But when I asked Bronwen she said to go ahead and see what they wrote. I asked them if they were comfortable writing about a sad day. There was a pause, then Nthabiseng said, "Yes, that is all right," so they did.

Lance wrote about being ignored by friends outside of Beka School. He once again wrote only about forty words, concluding, "I was not as happy as Larry, and the day was as cold as ice."

Anele wrote on the death of her teenage sister's infant son Simpiwe (whom she called her brother): "My granny told me and she said, 'please don't cry,' at night we sang and sang, my sister was crying I wanted to cry too but I couldn't."

Nthabiseng wrote about the day her friend Nhlanhla left school at the end of last year: "I thought he was going to be my best friend forever but he left me behind. Nhlanhla was so kind, humble and helpful I'm going to miss Nhlanhla a lot. I love Nhlanhla as I love myself. He was a good boy." (Bronwen later said of Nhlanhla: "He is a blind boy from a shack in Daveyton [east of Johannesburg] who started high school this year.")

I thought the invitation to write about a sad day might bring out memories of being burned. But I later found out that most of the kids were burned as infants or toddlers. Only Munashe wrote about that day:

> *A sad day for me is when I got burned. I got burned when I was still 12 years old. My Granny was sleeping in her own room. Clare and I were sleeping in our own room and the boys were sleeping in they own room. At 9:00, the girl room started the fire. My granny didn't hear the fire. Then someone who was passing nearby our house he saw the fire and he came to help us. Then he called my granny and my granny came then she started to call the ambulance and the ambulance came to fach us to the hospital and we stay there like 6 moth. It was sad. I will never forget it again.*

Portrait: Munashe Anderson

Munashe Anderson, age fourteen, is an orphan from Zimbabwe who came to Children of Fire with her cousin Clara, both severely burned from a fire that broke out in the family hut. Munashe's mother died when Munashe was nine years old and her only brother died three years later when he ate from an open container of peanut butter that he had found by a rural shop. The container had been laced with rat poison to kill vermin.

After her mother's death, Munashe was looked after by a cousin who has two children of her own. Munashe slept on the floor of the family hut about thirty-five kilometers outside of Harare in an area known as Snake Park. Munashe and Clara were sleeping together when the roof of the thatched hut caught fire and collapsed on them. No one knows how the fire started, perhaps by the wind carrying a spark. The girls were pulled from the fire. Their burns were so severe that they were hospitalized for ten months in Parirenyetwa Government Hospital, Harare, before being discharged.

When the girls came to Children of Fire, Bronwen wrote on the website: "No child should have to live like this." Each girl needed major reconstructive surgery of the hands, arms, and eyes that was not available in Zimbabwe. Poor skin grafting in Zimbabwe had in fact pulled Munashe's hand back. Clara's left hand was and still is so deformed that it looks like she is holding her right hand upside-down and backwards in her left hand. The girls will need multiple operations before they will be able to button a button, hold a toothbrush, or tie their shoes.

Their rehabilitation will also require thermoplastic splinting and pressure garments to position their arms correctly, a challenge made more urgent because as the girls continue to grow their arms will grow longer into the wrong positions. Thermoplastic splinting (molded plastic splints), after or in place of surgery, immobilizes and supports the injured joints. For many children of fire, splinting takes months to allow the burned scar tissue to lengthen. Munashe had arm surgery, other surgeries, and splinting performed at Chris Hani Baragwanath Hospital shortly after she arrived.

Munashe Anderson

Munashe and Clara require ongoing eye care as well. In the months after the fire, Munashe lost sight in one eye due to lack of eyelid reconstruction, ointments, and eye patches. Like Anele, when Munashe and Clara first came to Children of Fire, they slept with eyes and mouths open due to skin contractions. Munashe's eye is slightly better now that Children of Fire obtained a scleral shell (for 18,000 rand, or $1,650) that was inserted over her damaged left eye.

Treatment for Munashe's injuries will not end any time soon. Bronwen anticipates that Munashe and Clara will live at Children of Fire for two years before returning to their extended family in Zimbabwe.

"The only change in plans would be if someone offered to adopt Munashe," she said. "That's highly unlikely because she's not sweet and cute enough in that candyfloss-pink world of do-gooders and most of all, not young enough. If only people could see the real beauty inside these children, they'd be hammering on my door for the chance to adopt."

I know what Bronwen means. When I first saw the children I couldn't help but see them as disfigured, unattractive. But as I got to know them I came to see them as truly beautiful, inside *and* out. Knowing who they were—their charms and quirks of personality—I also came to appreciate the specifics of their faces and bodies, even—perhaps especially—the scars which marked them as individuals.

This was especially true of Munashe. At first I could not see past her disfigurement. And the clinical pictures that Bronwen posted on the website revealed in more detail the severe burns on Munashe's head, face, arms, legs, and torso. But Munashe is so bubbly and irrepressible that her inner nature makes her beautiful. And, in fact, she really is beautiful.

I sent my wife, Kathy, a picture of Nthabiseng and Munashe in costume. Nthabiseng is lovely: her skin perfect, smile bright, eyes aglow. Yet it is Munashe about whom Kathy remarked, "Oh, she's beautiful!" Small wonder that Munashe's name in her home language of Shona means "God is with you."

Munashe and Nthabiseng in costume

7

Why Poor Children Get Burned

MY GROWING INTEREST IN the children piqued my curiosity about their injuries and treatments, so on the days I was not with the children I researched child burn injuries worldwide. Among other things, I wanted to know the ways in which the children of fire are similar to or different from other children who have been badly burned, especially in Africa and the developing world.

In one respect, Anele, Munashe, and Clara *are* similar to other children: they were burned in highly flammable close quarters—a shack or a hut, the most common site for child burn injuries and deaths in sub-Saharan Africa. Throughout Africa, poor people build their shacks or huts and squeeze into densely-crowded informal settlements.[1] These small homes usually consist of one or two rooms with a room divider made of flammable curtains or tall boards. Water is available only from a common water tap, often not close to the dwelling. Despite increasing electrification in some countries, including South Africa, most residents of informal settlements use candles, paraffin stoves, or wood-fired stoves for cooking and heating because the costs of electricity and electrical appliances are too high.[2]

1. Van Niekerk et al., "Area Characteristics and Determinants," 118.
2. Teo, "Comparison of the Epidemiology," 805, and Schwebel et al.,

In addition, the ongoing mass migration of Africans to urban areas adds to the overcrowding in informal settlements.[3] About 30 percent of these households are headed by a female, most of whom are poor and unemployed. (In South Africa, the poverty rate among female-headed households is about 60 percent.)[4] These women often have so much to do in the home—cooking, cleaning, and informal selling of crafts or goods—that they cannot always attend to all of their children, especially curious toddlers learning to explore the world.[5] Thus, small children are often left unsupervised or in the care of older (but not much older) children; it is not unusual in developing countries for an eight-year-old to be looking after a two-year-old.[6] Worldwide, the youngest children are most susceptible to burn injuries and even death. According to the World Health Organization (WHO), infants have the highest death rates, while those between ages ten and fourteen have the lowest.[7] (In one year, 60 percent of all pediatric burn admissions at Red Cross Children's Hospital in Cape Town were under the age of two.) Most of these children were of low socioeconomic status and came from informal settlements.[8] In short: the smallest African children, living in crowded squatter camps with exhausted mothers, are highly susceptible to getting seriously injured from a burn.

Anele, Munashe, Clara, and the other children of fire, while seriously injured, were fortunate to have survived. WHO reports that worldwide more than 95,000 children under the age of 20 die from burns each year. That's on average a child dying from burn injury *every five or six minutes.* Incidences of burn-related child deaths are disproportionately concentrated in low-income and middle-income countries in Southeast Asia (especially India, Bangladesh, and Indonesia) and sub-Saharan Africa. Mortality rates due

---

"Paraffin-related Injuries in Low-income," 704.

3. Albertyn et al., "Pediatric Burn Injuries," 605–7.

4. Van Niekerk et al, "Area Characteristics and Determinants," 121–22.

5. Ibid., 118.

6. Albertyn et al., "Pediatric Burn Injuries," 607.

7. World Health Organization, "World Report on Child Injury," 81.

8. Teo, "Comparison of the Epidemiology," 802.

to fire-related burns are eleven times higher in sub-Saharan Africa than in the Americas—the highest pediatric burn mortality in the world.[9] Dr. Ashley Van Niekerk, a leading pediatric burns researcher at the South African Medical Research Council, put it simply: "Burn injuries are a serious global health threat to young children."[10]

9. World Health Organization, "World Report. on Child Injury," 80.

10. Van Niekerk et al., "Caregiver Experiences, Contextualizations and Understandings," 236.

8

February 20: "I Sing Myself"

SINCE I HAD BROUGHT to South Africa a book of Walt Whitman's poems, it seemed only natural that his epic poem "Song of Myself" could inspire the children to write about their lives. I told them briefly about Whitman and then handed out the following excerpts from "Song of Myself," which we read in turns:

> I celebrate myself, and sing myself,
> And what I assume, you shall assume,
> For every atom belonging to me as good belongs to you.
> . . . And I know that the hand of God is the promise of my own,
> And I know that the spirit of God is the brother of my own,
> And that all the men ever born are also my brothers, and the women my sisters,
> And that a kelson of the creation is love . . ..[1]

When we finished reading I asked the children to write their own "Song of Myself." If they liked any lines from Whitman, or simply got stuck, they could use those. I also told them they would read their poems outside on the driveway and I would film them with the new camera I had just bought.

---

1. Whitman, "Whitman's Manuscript," 28, 31–32.

I could tell as they settled down to write that they were engaged. Whitman seemed to call forth a quality of expression they might not have otherwise achieved. I heard this quality as soon as they started reading.

Anele read first, capturing Whitman's proud and unapologetic spirit:

> I celebrate myself, and sing myself
> I am proud of myself,
> I am proud of my culture
> no one can tell me who i am.
> And i know that the spirit
> of God is the brother of my own
> I can sing
> I can dance,
> I know my strength.
> I really celebrate myself.
> I am not ashamed of my self
> people can laugh at me
> as long as I know my self
> and I don't care what
> people say about me.

Munashe's poem focused on her pride in learning to speak, write, and read English:

> I am proud of myself that
> I can sing. I can sing like a bird.
> I can dance like a rat.
> I am proud of myself that
> I can talk English and I can write it down and I can read some
> of words.
> I came here without noing English.
> I didn't no how to say one words in English.
> I didn't no how to write and I didn't no how to read.
> but now I am proud of myself because
> I can do all of that with words.

Munashe can indeed "do all of that with words" as this writing showed how far she'd come with her English in just two years at Children of Fire. But I wondered about her phrase "dance like a rat." When she read the line and nobody laughed, I realized that I was the only one not getting it. She and the others had seen a rat dancing!

Dikeledi's poem moved me the most. Quiet but confident, wearing a salmon-colored hoodie to cover her tissue expander, she read:

> I celebrate myself, and sing myself
> I love myself as I love the world
> But I do not talk of the beginning and the end.
> And for me I always want to be free but the world is like that no
> one can be free like a bird.
> I care about myself, and I can sing and dance.
> And one day I will be on stage singing like an angel.
> I have practeced so long to learn to read and
> now I am writing a poem about myself.
> You should not feed on the specters in books,
> you shall not look through my eyes either, nor take things from me,
> you shall listen to all sides
> and filter them from yourself.
>
> This world is yours don't be scared.
> No one is dissatisfied, not one is demented with the mania
> of owning things,
> Not one kneels to another, nor to his kind that lived thousands
> of years ago,
> Not one is respected
> or unhappy over the whole earth.
> And I am telling you this earth god made it for us.
> And I know that the hand
> of God is the promise of my own,
> And I know that the spirit of God is the brother of my own.
> And for me to be a singer I have to work hard for that
> and I could be a singer with the help of God.

And a keelson of the creation is love!
I LOVE MY SELF
AS I LOVE GOD.　　　　　　I Love The World.

When she finished reading, the other children broke into applause. Dikeledi's poem seemed to mark a breakthrough—not for its quality, though she achieved by accident or design some striking effects—but because she took writing, the *act* of writing, more seriously than anyone had to that point. And though she borrowed much from Whitman, her poem truly was a song of herself—her expression of love (including self-love), as well as a song *about* song, her dream that one day she will "be on stage singing like an angel."

Portrait: Dikeledi Mboko

Dikeledi Mboko was born in Lesotho, the "mountain kingdom" nation geographically inside South Africa, and brought to Children of Fire when she was eight years old. Dikeledi is an orphan, one of three siblings whose mother is dead and father unknown. The children had no income and survived only on occasional food parcels. Dikeledi was brought to Children of Fire by a social worker seeking homes for the three siblings living on their own. While the other two were placed with families, no one took in Dikeledi. She had been burned on her head, hands, and feet. After coming to Children of Fire, she had hand surgery and various tissue expanders in her scalp, with limited success.

Dikeledi Mboko

Not yet twelve years old, Dikeledi was one of the younger members of our *Macbeth* group, yet one of the strongest readers and writers. I could give her difficult parts, like Banquo or Lady Macbeth, and she would sight-read Shakespeare with only a few errors. One time I accidently burst into what I thought was a storage room inside the school, only to find Dikeledi reading for an elderly woman who tutored voluntarily.

Dikeledi likes to sing and sings well. She often takes the lead part in the call-and-response songs the girls sing together. I always admired Dikeledi's sensitivity and thoughtfulness. She remains an orphan whom Bronwen dearly hopes someone will adopt.

9

February 24: "We Have the Same Souls"

Two "new" members joined the group today, each ten years old and new only to me because they are returning to Children of Fire after some time away.

Zanele Jeza has a masklike face of scars and a raspy voice. Quiet and small for her age, she does good, thoughtful work. Zanele is the youngest of six children in a family from Soweto, the sprawling township southeast of Johannesburg. When she was twenty-one months old, she was accidentally burned by her mother pouring a pot of floor polish made from hot wax and paraffin. Zanele's face and legs were badly burned, though her trunk, neck, and hands were left unscathed. She was hospitalized at Chris Hani Baragwanath Hospital for four months. Zanele has at times worn a face mask "pressure garment" to release contractions in her face which make it difficult for her to eat and smile.

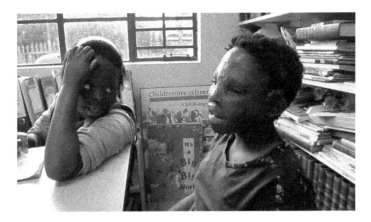

Anele and Zanele

Nelson-Ernest Tshabalala also has a mask of scars, but in contrast to Zanele he is not quiet! A wonderful mimic, Nelson joins Lance as the second comic in the group, able to make us all laugh. As a five-year-old, he was severely burned when the family house burnt down, killing Nelson's mother. Nelson suffered injuries to his face, scalp, stomach, and to his hands, which developed severe contractures. He has been an off-and-on resident at Children of Fire for five years.

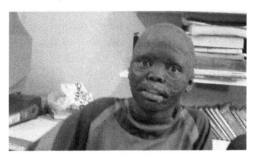

Nelson Tshabalala

Nthabiseng, our "one-legged Macbeth" as Bronwen calls her, returned from hospital today after a week away for hand surgery. Soon she will be fitted for a prosthetic leg. She asked about the "sad day" writings she had missed. Munashe told her briefly of her writing about the day she was burned, which launched Nthabiseng into a passionate monologue about how, though she is burned, she is proud of herself and is no different from other children, aside from appearance. I asked her if she would repeat what she'd just said as I filmed her. She agreed and soon the others joined in. Here is what they said.

> *Nthabiseng: People like to ask me, How do I feel I'm burnt, neh? Me, I'm telling them I feel happy because there are people that like me and they understand that even though I'm burnt and I'm not looking like them, I'm proud of myself because other people love me.*

> *Anele: People like to ask me how do I feel when I'm burned. Some of them I tell them I feel great and I'm proud of myself, so I don't need to feel ashamed. Then they ask me how did I get burned. And then I explain that I got burned when I was three months. Then they will be saying, "How does the fire feel like if you get burned?" And I will be like, "I don't know how does it feel like. I don't know if I was crying or laughing or jumping on top of the bed, because I was young, so I don't know how does it feel like." And I'm proud of myself.*

> *Nthabiseng: I'm glad that you are proud of yourself, neh, because God created us and we are the same. God didn't mean that if you are burned people mustn't love you. We have to love one another, because he created us the same. We are the same. We have the same souls-it doesn't matter just because we are burned as children of fire.*

> *Lance: As they say, we are all equal!*

> *Dikeledi: People ask me how old was I when I was burned and how do I feel. And I just tell them that I feel great because I know I am just the same as them. I'm just equal as them. It's just because I am burned I am not the same. But that doesn't mean that. And I know that when I go in the road and people look and laugh at me, I don't feel bad because I know I am just the same as them. It's just that I*

have scars on my face and my legs and my body. So I don't mind about them what they say.

Nelson: People ask me why am I burned, because I am going in a school where people are not burned, and me I'm the only one who is burned. And they make fun out of me, but I do not mind them. They must know that I am the same as them but it's just that we are burned. And they feel ashamed and say, "Oh no man. Your face. What happened to your scars?" And some of us who are blind they think that we can see, but we can't see, and then they bang us on things and they like hit our heads. They are like playing with our heads.

Nthabiseng: They say that all that glitters is not gold.

Nthabiseng and Lance together: We are all equal!

Lance: We are not monsters. We are like you.

Nthabiseng: God loves us. We should love one another. Don't only love yourself. They said love yourself as you love your neighbor. Don't just love me because I am burned. Just love me from your heart with open arms. And please, don't be ashamed of us. "Oh, this child!" No. Just to get me happy? Just pretend like I'm not burned. We are the same. We are like sisters and brothers.

Anele: That's why sometimes we go on TV. We tell our stories about how did we get burned. And please don't feel ashamed of us because we are all equal. It's just that we got scars.

Nelson: Yeah, you should donate!

Nthabiseng: Yes, just to help us build our charity because Children of Fire helps us. We have bad situations at home-people are looking at us. I came here somehow. Because of Bronwen, Children of Fire helped me a lot and I understand my situation now.

Munashe: Yeah, Bronwen helped a lot, a lot.

Nthabiseng: If there's no Bronwen we are not going to be here. We are not going to be nice, smoothy ladies. And now look it [holding up bandaged arm]. I have a proper operation now. They're going to fix it. It's going to be proper because of Bronwen. If there is not Children of Fire I was going to be somewhere else, because people are teasing at me, telling me, "Oh Nthabiseng." Now when I am going home, they won't believe. I would like to thank Bronwen and I would like to thank Children of Fire, to be honest, and God, to just, you know, to help us through the charities.

Dikeledi: And some kids, when they see us they start to cry, which hurts us. And then after that as we look at them they are scared like insects. We are not one of them. We know that we are burnt, we have scars, and we don't care about our scars because we know that we are still alive and we are still human beings.

Anele: At my school they used to tease me and always I will cry. And then the teacher will be like, "If they tease you, may you please come and tell me? I will deal with them." And then they will tease me. Sometimes I don't tell teacher because I feel like I don't have friends at school at my home. I didn't know who I am when I was at home. Since I came to Children of Fire I did my operations. Now I know who I am: I am a real Anele.

The children concluded with the familiar chant led by Nthabiseng:

Thank you [clap-clap-clap]
Very much [clap-clap-clap]
Keep it up [clap-clap-clap]
And shine!
Another one [clap-clap-clap]
Just like that [clap-clap-clap]
Ee-yoh ee-yooooh!

Thank you Professor Martin! And Bronwen!

10

February 25: "The Ere the Set of Sun"

EACH OF THE CHILDREN has settled into his or her own part in *Macbeth* by now, despite frequent absences due to one or more of them going in for surgery.

They begin the play with thunder by pounding on the table while the witches—Lance, Feleng, and Munashe—sound a demonic high-pitched laughter, their heads thrust back and voices pitched skyward.

Then I give the signal to Lance who begins with gusto as Witch 1: "When shall we three meet again? In thunder, lightning, or in rain?"

Feleng as Witch 2: "When the hurly-burly's done, When the battle has lost and won." (The line is actually "When the battle *is* lost and won," but after repeated attempts to correct Feleng I let the error go.)

Munashe as Witch 3: "That will be the ere the set of sun."

"No!" we all yell. "It's 'ere.' Not '*the* ere.'" (Munashe eventually corrected her mistake after accepting our criticism with her usual good humor.)

Lance and Feleng have gotten quite good at calling on their familiars, those spirits that supposedly helped witches perform black magic. Lance's familiar is Graymalkin the cat; Feleng's is Paddock the toad. At one point, Bronwen had a professional film crew capture the kids in rehearsal as part of a larger video project for Children of Fire. For props she brought out a rubbish bin as the witches' cauldron, a toy animal as Paddock the toad, and—shockingly—a stuffed fox as Graymalkin. Bronwen told me she raised pet foxes in England, though this wasn't one of them. For the famous scene in Act IV when the witches concoct their potent stew, she brought out a long, flexible plastic snake. When Munashe saw the snake, she ran frightened to the edge of the property. For several minutes Bronwen and Munashe faced each other in a standoff, Bronwen telling Munashe she must come back and face her fear, and Munashe not moving. Finally Munashe came back, assured that the snake was plastic and that she didn't have to look at it. "This is good for her," Bronwen said to me. "Give her forty minutes and she'll be over it."

The children love the goriness of *Macbeth*, beginning with Lance saying as King Duncan, "What bloody man is that?" They also like hearing how Macbeth "unseamed" Macdonald and "fixed his head upon our battlements." When Lance realized just how deliciously gory the play was, he began to look for carnage throughout the script. After others left the room, he'd remain, his head buried in the text. He breathlessly reported to me one day that he'd stumbled upon the murder of Banquo—a boon to him but a surprise and sadness to the other children who'd grown fond of Macbeth's friend.

It isn't long before I realize that what we are performing is not so much *Macbeth* as *The Witches of Macbeth*. When our witches confront Macbeth with prophecies of his future ("All hail, Macbeth, that shalt be king hereafter!") they ham up it up, bowing low and sweeping their arms low in prostration. And when Banquo addresses them—"You seem to understand me / By each at once her chappy finger laying / Upon her skinny lips"—our three witches circle Banquo and Macbeth with fingers upon their lips, occasionally thrusting out their ghoulish faces. But most of all, our witches enjoy vanishing, running in ever widening circles on the driveway and screaming in delight. The little kids, watching through the gate, howl with laughter.

Chapter 11

February 27: "That's Touching!"

TODAY I HAD THE children focus on their hopes and dreams by asking them to imagine writing a letter in 2025 to anyone they cared to write, telling of their accomplishments. The concept of writing backwards from the future puzzled a couple of them, so I gave them the option of writing forward into the future, i.e. what they hoped to do with their lives in the next eight to ten years.

Lance eagerly took to the project, especially when I urged the children to use their imagination. He asked me what the most famous university in America was. Not wanting to literally spell out more than I had to while the other kids were writing, I thought Harvard but said "Yale." Then he asked where it was. Heavens, I thought, I am not about to spell Connecticut. So I said "near New York City." Then he wanted to know a "famous" primary school. I told him I attended Central School, and when he asked where, I said, "Just put it in Los Angeles." He liked that and wrote it down.

Nelson and Feleng seemed to be interested in burying each other. Feleng wanted to know how to spell funeral, and when I asked why, he said that in ten years he was going to attend Nelson's funeral. This was darkly funny of course but not good for class morale, so I put a stop to it by saying we were not going to write about any funerals. That didn't seem to faze Feleng, so I said, "We'll be reading these to Bronwen."

"Reading these to Bronwen, yo!" he murmured.

He looked down at what he'd written and seemed to calculate if he could read *any* of it to Bronwen. He wrote a few sentences, then turned to his soccer magazine as usual, writing far less than the others.

Munashe read first. She'd written a lovely note to her "mother" about how she and Clara were doing so well in 2025 that she wished her mother could see them. I happened to know Munashe's mother had died, so I found this moving. (Bronwen later suggested that Munashe may have been thinking of Clara's mother, i.e. her aunt, as "mother.") When Munashe finished I said, "Thank you. That was quite touching." Lance picked up on the word: "Yes, Munashe, that was *touching*." When some of them laughed, I simply said again how much I liked her story.

Lance then read about his life in a letter to Nthabiseng: graduating from Yale near New York City, then moving to Los Angeles where he taught grade 2 at Central School, all while starting a hip-hop career on the side. Next came Anele's story, and it too was touching, so I said so. Now they all joined in to mock the word, even the usually serious Dikeledi, who read next. When she finished reading her thoughtful and well-written letter, I didn't need to say I found it touching—which it was—because they all said it for me.

"That was touching, Dikeledi." "Yes, really touching!"

I had seen this before: one of the kids writing or saying something beautiful and personal, only to be mocked, if lovingly, by the others. Yet the kids are far less mean to each other than I imagine most kids to be. More than that, they are resilient. If teased, they brush it off. Only rarely do they flash at each other in anger.

When Feleng read, I could see from his notebook that he'd written about ten lines. Yet he read for two to three minutes, making most of it up on the spot, his eyes drifting from the page. Munashe caught him out. "You are not reading!" she said in her machine-gun burst of language.

I thanked him for his story and we moved on to little Zanele, sweet and raspy-voiced. I asked the others to be quiet so we could listen. Zanele's writing *was* touching. She'd written a letter to Nthabiseng, who was absent due to clerical training Bronwen had arranged for her. Zanele wrote how much she missed Nthabiseng—not in 2025, but on *this* day—because Nthabiseng "makes everything fun." I knew what was coming when Zanele finished, but I was powerless to stop it. "That's touching! That's touching!" But Anele, who can be moved to praise, said "Wow" and broke into applause. That silenced the others. Good for her.

Here are their letters from the future.

MUNASHE
To: My Lovely Mother
Dear Mother,

I miss you. I want to tell you the good news. I be come a doctor. And clara be come a teacher. that is not nice mother!? Mother I am in Botswana. I wish you will come to visit me and clara.

I still remember the days that you cooked for us the delicious food. Mother how is Father? Is he fine? Mother please tell him that I love him and my brother's and sister's I love them. And I will never forget them. And you too mother. I still remember the days I was going to school with my brother's and my sister's. it was nice days that I will never forget. And can you tell them that I love them please mother. And tell father that he must come to visit me please. Please mother tell my friends that I love them.

LANCE
27 February 2025
My future to Nthabiseng
Dear Nthabiseng

Hi it's me Lance from the past do you remember me. I just want to say I just pass metrick and I'm studying at yale university near New York City studying for a teacher teaching at a school called Central Primary School in Lass Angeles teaching grade 2 and grade 3 learners. Wait I do have some more I have just started being a hip hop singer. See you me and my wife are going to buy some nappies for our children and wait I have just bought a new house because my wife smashed the windows because she said I was sleeping with a nother woman ha lol I didn't sleep with the lady and I told her so she got mad and smashed the windows. And wait just want to say my cd is out and it is called Dedication 4. So ya see you. Bye, From Ritch gang

ANELE

When I grow up I want to be a doctor i want to operate people I love takeing care of people I want to go to university to starde there. I want to have my own car I want to have a big car like Land Rover. And I love baby sitting changeing nepees, feeding and playing and when they are crying I can make them quiet and they will be sleeping quickly.

DIKELEDI

Once upon a time there was a little girl who dreamed of being a singer. And she lived in Lesotho with her sister and brothers. She lived with them because she didn't have a mother or father. And that little girl loved her parents very much. And when she did anything she thought of them (going to university, working hard and 'let her dream come true') . . . And this little girl she will have her future and will still not forget her mother's beautiful face and she will bless her wherever she goes and her sister and brothers.

After that girl lets her dream come true she will let people talk about her family she will not care about what they say she still remembers their faces even when she gets a new family she will not forget her family nor her dream . . . And she will like to be a singer in New York and if she gets a family she will bless the family she will have in the future and bless her old family.

NEW YORK! love you!

The afternoon ended with our visit to Bronwen's office to view the opening scenes from the 1996 film version of *Macbeth* on YouTube. We crowded around Bronwen's desk and watched a long opening battle scene in which Macbeth wades through soldiers in hand-to-hand combat until he reaches Macdonwald. Standing above him with sword in hand, Macbeth pauses, then thrusts the sword through Macdonwald as his men erupt in shouts of "Macbeth! Macbeth!" The kids were mesmerized.

In the next scene the three witches—two old hags and a misty-eyed young clairvoyant—meet on an eerie, windswept moonscape. The third witch, looking off into the distance, says: "That will be ere the set of sun." Munashe piped up: "That's me!"

12

March 1: "They Don't Shrink in the Rain"

Hlumelo, Perlucia, and Clara setting off

Today was a day I won't soon (or ever) forget. No fireworks, celebrations, or grand festivities. Just a hike with kids: a *three and-a-half mile hike in the rain* to Emmarentia Dam and the Johannesburg Botanical Gardens with thirteen children of fire and one volunteer.

When Bronwen told me about the picnic at the dam, I was eager to go. I wanted to spend fun time with the kids and see the dam and surrounding park which I knew only as a big green space on my Gauteng map. While we chatted she held Rien, a six-month-old baby boy from the Congo with serious facial and head burns just back from hospital. He kicked and kicked and made sweet bubbly noises through his mouth and looked affectionately at her with his one good eye, the other patched over.

I offered to drive the children to the park in two carloads.

"They are not being transported," Bronwen said, "they're walking. That's the whole point. They need the exercise."

"It looks like a long way on the map," I said.

"They can do it," she said. "They've done it before."

So today at 10:15 we set off on foot. It was raining, so Bronwen outfitted the kids with coats, anyone who wanted one. Perlucia and Hlumelo, both six years old and barely up to my waist, sported adult black raincoats that fell like formal dresses to their ankles.

Bronwen's adopted daughter, Dorah, also joined us. Dorah is the genesis of Children of Fire. The short version of this story is that Bronwen saved Dorah in infancy from almost certain death from horrific burn injuries to her face and head by insisting on Dorah's proper care in hospital. She later adopted Dorah and has arranged operations—about thirty so far—that have helped Dorah function. Dorah was the first of more than 400 children Bronwen has similarly helped after founding Children of Fire as a charitable trust in 1997. Dorah is legally blind and not able to speak, but she can hear and can convey her feelings, her basic needs (food, toilet, etc.) and, Bronwen says, her mischievous sense of humor. In any outing, Dorah must be escorted. When we started off, Feleng dutifully took her by the hand, but for most of the way she was escorted by Wendy, age eighteen, the other volunteer on the hike besides me. Dorah wore her prosthetic nose—the one Feleng identified for me earlier in the school kitchen.

Feleng, Dorah, and Wendy

To a non-South African like me this little walk to the park seemed a bit perilous: thirteen kids ages six to seventeen strung out along a tiny, narrow, muddy path next to a four-lane "main road" (i.e. highway) with cars zipping past at forty miles per hour in the opposite direction, splashing water from the rain. Some of the kids were wearing flip-flops. Nthabiseng hopped along on one leg and a crutch.

Feleng, Dikeledi (front), Dorah, Anele, Nthabiseng, Zanele (back)

But the children had done this before and were clearly happy just to be on the journey. Little Perlucia and Hlumelo held Clara's good hand, though neither of them has a fully functioning hand with all fingers intact. The group had several umbrellas, including a big multi-colored one that I took at one point, walking next to the road and holding it horizontally like a shield or weapon, ready to whack any car that came too close. Several times the kids broke into song—pop songs or Christian gospel music—led by Nthabiseng or Dikeledi. Later inside the park, when we came upon people setting up a big red tent for a birthday party and listening to a boom box blasting hip-hop, the kids broke into dance. Nthabiseng on her one leg did a *real* hip-hop.

Hip-hop dancers Anele, Loide, Nthabiseng

At an intersection outside the park, a craggy, sunburned white man was begging for change, a common sight at many intersections in Johannesburg, though most beggars are black men. "Oh great," I thought. "This guy is white and perfectly healthy, and these kids are disabled, black, and burned. What's his problem?" He looked stunned as he watched the children cross the street. He approached me.

"Who are these children? Where do they come from?"

I told him.

"God bless them," he said, looking at me with piercing blue eyes. "God bless them. I think I have problems, but look at them."

He kept yelling "God bless you!" at the children well after they had crossed the road.

Dorah, Wendy, Feleng, and I entered the park last, trailing the others by about fifty meters. Dorah began moaning. Wendy told me that meant she had to use the toilet. Loide, an older girl in grade 10, had pushed ahead with most of the smaller kids, so we yelled up to them to let them know we were stopping.

"That toilet is no good!" Loide yelled back. "She doesn't like it!"

"It can't be that bad," I said to Wendy. "Let me check it out."

I'd cleaned outdoor toilets while working for the parks department in high school so I have a pretty high tolerance for their stench and filth. I went in. Not so bad.

Feleng and Wendy brought Dorah to the toilet while I walked to the parking lot and watched a white woman herd seven dogs into her SUV. I waited for them about ten minutes. Later Bronwen told me that because Dorah doesn't have functioning fingers, she can't wipe herself. Others wipe her—in this case, Wendy. Shortly after we started off again, Dorah stopped, turned, and hugged Wendy, making a high-pitched wailing sound. I thought maybe she was tired or hungry or wanted to go home.

"Why is she doing that?" I asked Feleng.

"She loves her," he said.

And no wonder. Wendy: faithful and patient. Wendy, Dorah's friend.

After that I caught up with Perlucia and Hlumelo in their dresslike raincoats and walked with them. Bronwen calls them "our little Mr. and Mrs." because they look like a small old married couple: they are the same age and height and their scalps are scarred bald. They also play together, Perlucia giving orders and Hlumelo quietly following.

Perlucia was having trouble with her flip-flops; mud kept getting between her foot and flip-flop so that she slid as she walked. She stopped several times, wiped mud from her foot on the grass, then stepped back into her flip-flops and continued without comment. She liked the ducks in the pond, but when she approached they flew off. When the three of us came into a wooded area she looked up and said quietly to me, "Maybe the three witches live here!"

We arrived at the Botanical Gardens outdoor restaurant about two hours and fifteen minutes after departure. The girls sat quietly along one bench while Loide and Wendy brought out food. Nelson, Feleng, and I kicked a soccer ball. It was a nice and needed feast: sandwiches, eggs, bananas, apples, rolls, and muffins.

Watching some of the kids eat was poignant. They were handicapped by disability yet able to overcome it. Hlumelo, for example, with only a few fingers, held his food as best he could, but every now and then a chunk of sandwich fell to the pavement. Perlucia and Hlumelo shared their food and helped each other eat. It was, indeed, touching.

Wendy and Dikeledi took turns putting food into Dorah's mouth. She was able to eat most of the food, though some fell. Looking around I joked, "I hope the ducks find this—it's quite a feast we're leaving." But the children didn't leave a mess. When we finished, Wendy fetched a broom from the restaurant and swept as others cleaned the tables.

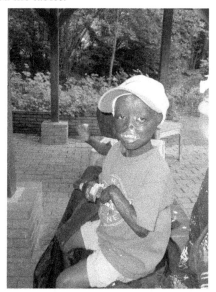

Hlumelo at lunch

Now it was time for *Macbeth*. I'd forgotten to bring my book, but I was not alone. In fact, only Nthabiseng brought hers, and she was the one most eager to perform scenes. We set up in a corner of the patio, vacant but for a group of four older people having lunch on the other side. Bronwen made sure we brought Nthabiseng's Viking helmet and Munashe's red-and-black witch's wig. Since Lance, our day schooler, was not with us, Nthabiseng took his role as Witch 1, joining Feleng and Munashe in the opening scene. I got my camera rolling as the three witches nailed it to great applause. In the next scene though, the children got into an argument about who was supposed to say what, leading to a funny moment when Nthabiseng read the messenger's speech to Macbeth, then turned around and responded as Macbeth.

The rain began to beat down harder on the patio roof, so I told the children I'd run back to the house to fetch my car and take them home in two trips. Walking and running on the way back I wondered when was the last time I'd walked seven miles—in the rain no less. But as I thought of the kids—Perlucia and Hlumelo plodding along in their soggy sandals and ankle-length trench coats, Nthabiseng hopping the whole way, Wendy and Dorah keeping on at the back—my trek seemed nothing. Bronwen sets the bar so high for these children that nothing seems impossible, or at least worth complaining about. Even when Perlucia pointed out to me her slippery flip-flops, that's all she meant—information, not a complaint.

I went as fast as I could, sure I was carrying out a rescue mission for these poor children, tired and wet in the rain. But when I returned with the car, they were singing! Dikeledi and Nthabiseng took turns leading a song in Sotho as the others sang, clapped, and swayed in response. The older children were having so much fun that they didn't even want to leave. So in my first trip I took Wendy, Loide, Dorah, and the little ones, leaving behind the "Macbethers." Loide went inside to thank the restaurant manager, which seemed unnecessary to me since he hadn't done anything except let us have some outdoor space. When I returned for the second group,

Nthabiseng *also* thanked the restaurant manager. It was just the sort of thing these kids had learned to do.

The older group kept singing all the way back in the car. After I dropped them off and returned to my room, I picked out five pictures I'd taken and posted them in my first-ever entry on Facebook, hoping to capture my sense of the day. The first person to respond wrote what I felt: "Amazing!"

Bronwen was less impressed. After reading my post, she wrote matter-of-factly in an email: "The kids quite often walk there and back; it's better without rain but they don't shrink in the rain." She added that walking in the rain was good practice for those going to Children of Fire's London site to await operations in England: "Dikeledi, Feleng, Dorah know the UK well; Nelson, Zanele, [and] Loide hope to travel to the UK this year."

13

March 4: "The Eye that I Got"

The kids' writings today were generally brief and uninspired, perhaps because my topic for them was uninspired: If you could be an animal, what animal would you be? Anele wrote that she would like to be a dog because "when the bad people come they can buyt them. No one can kill me easy and some of the dogs are beautiful some are not into buyting. Battins [Buttons, one of two house dogs] is a kind dog. And they eat everything that people eat."

Dikeledi wrote that the animal she'd like to be is a "unicorn" because a unicorn is "beautiful, has wings, and it's not scared because it is strong."

Dikeledi understood that unicorns aren't real (before she started writing she asked if she could write about a make-believe animal). Lance, however, was less informed. He wrote that his favorite animal is a "Dragon because it can fly, and it can blow fire and it stays in a very long tower looking after the princess." When one of the children told him that dragons aren't real, he refused to believe it. They turned to me to adjudicate. Lance was crestfallen to find out the truth. My sense is that as a day-schooler he watches far more TV than the others and perhaps can't always distinguish fact from fiction. He amended his writing to say that his favorite animal was now a dog.

Munashe asked if she could write on a different topic. When I asked her what that was, she said, "A happy day." I was pleased by her initiative, so I let her. This is what she wrote:

> Today it was a happy day for me. Hanne [Hannah, a volunteer] and I, we went to the hospital. The name of the hospital it was Jack Bernard. [Jack Bernard is an oculist.] I went to the hospital to get my eye. Then the doctor needed to make it until it was done. Then at 12:00 I was hungry as a wilf [wolf]. Then Hanne went to buy some food. She bought chips and bagger [burger] and some drinkes like coca cola. I saw the watch it was like this . . . and the eye that I got it was like this.

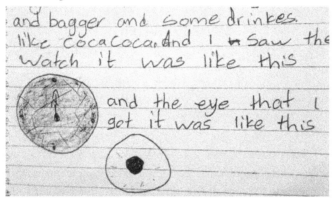

Munashe's drawing of her new eye

Munashe's new "eye" is actually a scleral shell, an ocular prosthesis worn over a blind or damaged eye. Munashe's eye socket had been "unsightly and unseeing," Bronwen said. Munashe's cousin Clara has the same injury. "But at 18,000 rand, a scleral shell can break easily," Bronwen said, "and a fourteen-year-old girl must prove she can look after it before we start with a younger one."

14

March 7: "I Love Her More than the Whole World"

TODAY WHILE WE WAITED for all of the children to arrive, I mentioned to Nelson and Zanele how much it had been raining lately. It was now raining again.

"That means the monkeys are getting married," Nelson said.

"Yes, the monkeys are getting married," Zanele repeated.

"Why do the monkeys get married when it rains?" I asked. "Is it because they are together up in the trees?"

"No," Nelson said, "that's just what you say when it rains: 'the monkeys are getting married.'"

"But why," I persisted. "Do the monkeys get married when it rains?"

"Because," he said, "they love each other!" (I should have known.)

When all were fully present and accounted for, I asked the children to write about a person they admired. They jumped right into the writing. I expected to see essays on mothers, teachers, or Bronwen, but as I looked around I saw Zanele and Munashe writing about Nthabiseng, and Nthabiseng writing about all of them! She read for us a paragraph listing her friends at Children of Fire, Bronwen, and me. I told her I wanted specific details on each of the persons she admired, thinking she might cut back the list. She looked up and said, "I am getting to that."

Feleng as usual "finished" first, followed not long after by Nelson. While the boys went outside, I stayed and waited for the girls. I could see we were in for a long haul.

Munashe held up her notebook and smiled: "Ah, this is good, from here to here. Two pages on Nthabiseng."

Nthabiseng responded: "I am going to write three pages on Munashe. Trust me." She read slowly as she wrote, the praise for Munashe spilling out word by word.

Munashe listened then went back to writing. At one point she interrupted herself: "I thought I forgot to spell pain," she laughed. "I still remember."

After thirty minutes I got up, encouraged the girls to keep going, and went outside where Feleng and Nelson were playing with blue beanbags. I took three beanbags and juggled them a few seconds before dropping one.

"Wow!" Feleng said.

I then taught the boys the first step of juggling as I'd learned it: throw-throw, catch-catch with just two beanbags. Feleng caught on quickly, but Nelson seemed to have trouble catching a beanbag. Only by looking closely did I realize why: his left hand was covered in a large cloth bandage from surgery.

Back inside the girls were still writing. While the children usually do well to write one page, Nthabiseng was going on eight! The others had written three or four, trying desperately to catch up.

At one point Nthabiseng looked around for the subject of her next paragraph. "Who's next?" She spotted Feleng, who had come in.

"Ah, Feleng," she said. "What have you ever done for me?"

He thought a moment. "Given you chocolates."

She considered this.

"I admire Feleng as a friend. That's it," she said, fixing him with a stare.

Finally she announced she was finished writing and read off the list of people she admired—all the other children, except one.

"You left out Zanele," I said. Zanele noticed this too. She looked up from her writing, quiet as usual, staring at Nthabiseng blankly, but sadly I think. Due to scarring, she cannot move her facial muscles and so can appear indifferent, but I could tell from her eyes that she was hurt.

"I did not write about Zanele, eh?" Nthabiseng said. She looked at Zanele across the table. "What have you ever done for me?"

"She is your friend!" Feleng said.

"Here," I said, "read this."

I handed her a notebook in which Zanele had written about Nthabiseng while Nthabiseng was in hospital for hand surgery. The assignment was the children's letter from 2025 to a friend. Nthabiseng looked at the notebook and read slowly, mouthing the words as she went:

> *Thursday, 27 February 2025*
> *To my friend Nthability*
>
> *Dear Nthabiseng,*
>
> *You have been a wonderful friend. I will like to say when I grow up I want to be a dentist. And what do you want to be in futere? The day you were not in class it was boring I could not write even when we playe at break time the game which is called B.f.f. vs Rich gang It was boring Lance, Clive, Nelson, Siyabong and Feleng were challenging Munashe, Clara, Dikeledi and I. I wish you were there to play with us. I wish when we grow up we can go visit some where else which you will like you Munashe Clive and I. Maybe we can go to london capetown or maybe we can go to visit your home or my home or Munashe or maybe we can go to Clives home.*
>
> *lots of Love from Zanele*

At the bottom of the page were two multi-colored hearts, one enclosing the words: *love you Nthability verry much.*

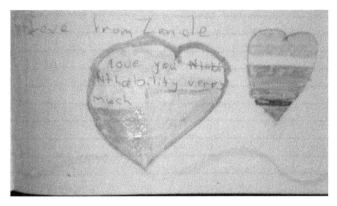

Zanele's note to Nthabiseng

Nthabiseng looked up at Zanele. "Oh, that is so beautiful Zanele. Come here." Zanele went to Nthabiseng who gave her a big hug, and that was that. Nthabiseng then launched into writing on Zanele.

What only Zanele knew and the rest of us were to find out later was that, at the very moment Nthabiseng had hurt her, Zanele was writing *another* tribute to Nthabiseng, which she later read out loud:

> *I admire Nthabiseng because she is beautiful, kind, helpful and sweet. I love her more than the whole wide world even my family knows that she is the kindest friend I like more than my friends at school I always dreamt bout her. She makes me feel like I am at home. We like to share any nice things we have. I really love her. Even on december I was crying because I wanted to phone her and speak. Even I would borou my fathers phone but my father did not have the school number I ask my sister she did not have airtime I even asked my mother her phone was out of battery and I would cry.*

Finally, all the girls had finished. I asked if we could have a reading in the big room and invite the little kids. Nthabiseng said yes, so we did.

Nthabiseng assumed master of ceremony duties, speaking to the five little kids and me on the couch, as Hlumelo and Perlucia perched on my knees. Nthabiseng announced that Professor

Martin had asked them to write about a person they admired and she explained what "admired" meant. Then she read her essay, a long, full tribute to the others and her love for them. At one point she looked at Nelson and said: "Nelson, I love you."

"Yo!" he said, embarrassed.

When she finished reading, Nelson said "touching," his sarcasm perhaps masking how he felt. His own essay was memorable for the humor with which it concluded:

> I admire Nthabiseng because she has been the greatest pearson in the whole school in the night she will give me some juice and bread then we will go to bed. Nthabiseng is the best because she will always stand for me I will never forget her never even when I am old and she will never forget me.

> I wish you the best Nthabiseng and may all your dreams come true only the good dreams. Pleas Nthabiseng do not cheat on your boy friend pleas. And remember that I will come to your house with my wife to give you R 30,000 in cash. So please do not forget me.   Nelson the Vice Mangure, Agent N1

The children laughed at his offer of 30,000 rand, even the little ones.

"Is that thirty thousand one time, or thirty thousand every time you see her?" I asked.

"It's thirty thousand every day!"

"Hey!" Nthabiseng said.

The reading ended up being one very long tribute from the other children to Nthabiseng, the eldest and their leader. Here, for example, is Munashe's:

> I admire Nthabiseng and I respect her as the way I respect my mother I take Nthabiseng as my sister and as my B.F.F. Best Friend Forever. And I love her as I love the world. And she is my friend. I remember the day that [I] went to the hospital of [for] operation on my hands she helped me to eat and bath and she was take to the office. That day I will never ever forget on my life. Sometimes she will shout [at] me but I will never forget what she

> *did to me. Nthabiseng she is such a beautiful girl and she helps a lots through a painful, even [when] I go to Zimbabwe I will tell my family about her. She is such a kind girl and I love her and she is my sister and I will talk about her everywhere I will go. I don't know what to do when she is not here. I feel like cry[ing] but I have nothing to do. Nthabiseng, My Sister*

For the record, my invitation to write about the person they admired resulted in Dikeledi writing five pages on eighteen people, Munashe writing seven pages on fourteen people, and Nthabiseng writing eight pages on twenty people. I had no idea they could write so much!

As the girls tired during their marathon writing session, their tributes grew shorter and shorter, often just a sentence on the person's qualities. But even after an hour of writing, they still expressed something genuine. Munashe wrote about Bronwen: *"I admire Mama because she is helping me to do my oparation. if it not mama nobody was going to help me like mama. I love you mama. I [am] really thankful mama. I will never forget you you are my mother for ever."*

What the children lacked in punctuation they poured out with their hearts. I felt deeply that I was in the midst of a loving family.

The afternoon ended at six o'clock, after more than two hours of writing and reading, with Nthabiseng leading us in another chorus of "I want to thank you"—clap-clap-clap—"very much!"

Nthabiseng impressed me that day by her leadership and by how beloved she was. When I came back to the office I said to Bronwen: "Nthabiseng strikes me as really coming into her own, I mean as a leader."

"I should hope so," Bronwen said. "She's the oldest."

Portrait: Nthabiseng Nkashe

Nthabiseng Nkashe

Zanele is right: Nthabiseng has Nthability. She's shown resilience and courage and a spirit for life ever since she came to Children of Fire.

Nthabiseng is from Lichtenberg in Northwest Province about 200 kilometers west of Johannesburg. As a baby she was dropped in a fire by an epileptic aunt.

"She has never walked properly, though she could have if people had taken the right decisions at the time," Bronwen said. "Her leg was savable. She would have only lost the front of the toes."

Instead, when Nthabiseng came to Children of Fire at age fifteen her skinny legs were "bent up really tight, kind of fixed up behind her," Bronwen said. "If the leg hadn't been welded the way it was, she'd have had the pleasure of running and walking. There's no way to quantify that."

Nthabiseng also had a large open wound which she covered with a sock.

"No social worker, no doctor even bothered to look," Bronwen said. "The poor child was dressing her own leaking leg wound with an old torn sock and a shabby bandage."

Bronwen had been working to get Nthabiseng to Children of Fire for more than two years, including a period when she was phoning social workers every day.

When Nthabiseng finally arrived, Bronwen took her to three hospitals in the first week. One surgeon saw that Nthabiseng's condition was urgent. In addition to her leg, her hip, abdomen, and hand were injured. Her left leg would have to be amputated, after which doctors would operate again so that the leg stump pointed in the right direction and could be fitted for a prosthetic leg.

At first Nthabiseng attended school by lying prone with several cushions under her chest to try to put pressure on her leg stump and realign it. Her ability—or *nthability*—to get around on one leg is little short of phenomenal. Sometimes she simply drops her crutch and hops full speed as fast or faster than others. One time she saw me from a distance on the road and took off in a one-legged sprint, leaving Dikeledi and Anele huffing to catch up. Another time I was having dinner outside at a local restaurant when I felt a tap on the shoulder. It was Nthabiseng whizzing by.

Nthabiseng's new leg is brown like her skin. In the beginning it felt heavy and awkward to her. The first time I saw it she'd propped it up against the table in our classroom, like an avant-garde piece of art. Each day she practiced walking—slowly, determinedly—the three blocks from school to office and back again, stopping every few feet to catch her breath and wipe sweat from her brow.

What Bronwen wrote on the website about Nthabiseng when she first met her has proved true: "She seems very stoic and determined by nature. She is a sweet girl and we will try to do what we can."

Nthabiseng has made it this far. With her "Nthability," I think she will be just fine.

15

Burn Treatment and Prevention in the Developing World

THE POOR MEDICAL RESPONSE to Nthabiseng's original burn injury is not uncommon in sub-Saharan Africa. While developed countries have made great strides in the prevention and treatment of burns, the same cannot be said of the developing world, especially Africa, because of a far different set of socioeconomic realities: far fewer medical resources, inadequate health and safety regulations, insufficient caregiver knowledge about burn prevention, and poorer access to electrical power and water.[1]

If a child in Africa is burned, the options for care are usually not good. In sub-Saharan Africa, outside of a few countries such as Nigeria and South Africa, hospitals do not have burn units. Those that do have burn units lack basic resources such as food, drugs, equipment, and sometimes even drinking water. Most burn care in Africa occurs in rural health centers or district hospitals where treatment is often limited to administering tetanus shots and antibiotics, caring for minor burn wounds, and providing analgesic tablets, vitamins, and iron.[2] And because treatment is

---

1. Parbhoo et al., "Burn Prevention Programs for Children," 165.
2. Albertyn et al., "Pediatric Burn Injuries," 608.

usually provided in trauma or general wards, patients are exposed to infection. Skin grafts can also be delayed for weeks due to inadequate operating time or limited blood availability in countries with high HIV/AIDS rates.

Mortality under these conditions is high. While American or European patients with burn wounds exceeding up to 90 percent of total body surface area (TBSA) can now survive, African patients exceeding 45 percent TBSA rarely survive. Young children with as little as 20 percent TBSA often die.[3]

Burn care in South Africa is better than in the rest of Africa, largely due to improved practices at major hospitals in Johannesburg, Durban, Cape Town, and other urban areas. South Africa can, at its best, offer an integrated system of care involving surgeons, occupational therapists, physiotherapists, and social workers.

South Africa has also made some progress in burn prevention by enacting legislation requiring safer standards for products such as paraffin (kerosene) stoves and candleholders. Short radio messages teach families and communities to recognize child burn risks and to organize child supervision when possible. Home safety demonstrations show people how to create a safer environment in shacks and small huts by raising cooking fires on bricks or stones, guarding open fires by using fire grids, and safely storing flammable substances.

Children of Fire performs "safety plays," such as the one they performed for about 200 children in the historically black African township of Alexandra shortly after a fire swept across the N1 highway from upscale Sandton. Anele played a child who got caught in a fire, Loide her mother, Feleng her father, and Zanele the ambulance. Dikeledi played a well-informed neighbor who stopped people from putting butter and toothpaste on the burn wounds. In the play, Anele was saved, treated with cold running water, and taken to hospital. After the play the children presented safety tips that they also publicize in radio and television adverts and in a safety awareness DVD, such as "Don't leave children in

3. Ibid.

charge of other children," "Put a candle inside a jar of sand," and "Teach children how to escape their home."

The play is an example of how Bronwen makes sure the children do not see themselves as victims of burn injuries, but empowered to help prevent such injuries from happening to others. In this way, Nthabiseng is representative: she came to Children of Fire unable to walk, and she became the leader of children, teaching others how to avoid the fate of fire that befell them all.

16

March 10: "Anon"

OUR WITCHES ARE THE most perfect and imperfect of witches. They might seem witchy by their scars and disfigurement and by the wicked, eerie noises they make around the cauldron. But their hearts are just too pure for them to be really good witches. Plus, as actors they don't know their motivation! This became all too clear when I invited two actor friends, Xolani Ngesi and Mongezi Ncwadi, to work with them.

I'd gotten to know Xolani and Mongezi in Cape Town when I was on a previous sabbatical teaching at University of Cape Town and they were performing a show at the Baxter Theatre called *Hungry Road*. I'd sat in on a few rehearsals because I wanted to learn about new forms of theatre in South Africa.

Looking back I realize that one of the performances of *Hungry Road* had a connection to a major fire. One evening the actors took the show to a high school gymnasium where about 100 people had been living while the city scrambled to find housing for them. A massive fire had swept through an informal settlement four months earlier, displacing thousands of people (one estimate put the number at 10,000). Inside the gymnasium the people had formed a little village, with small avenues leading through family residences that were often not more than a bed, dresser, and radio.

Mongezi, Xolani, and another actor performed in their home language of Xhosa for an appreciative audience. (At one point an older woman on the way to the kitchen intervened in an argument between the actors!)

In the months and years following I'd visit Mongezi and Xolani and their colleague, Zwai Mgijima, in New Brighton, their home township outside Port Elizabeth that is also home to their mentor, the stage and film actor Winston Ntshona. I even wrote a comedic play for them called *Fly Bhisho*, based on the true story of the Bhisho Airport outside of King Williams Town that for several years had twenty-nine paid employees but no airplanes. My friends graciously workshopped a few scenes with me and just as graciously never brought the play to light. Mongezi and Xolani were now in Jo'burg at The Market Theatre for a six-week run of *Ukutshona ko Mendi . . . Did We Dance*, the story of the sinking of the troopship *SS Mendi* during World War I in 1917 off the Isle of Wight, when more than 600 African men from Pondoland in the Eastern Cape lost their lives.

I know Mongezi and Xolani to be fun guys so I thought the afternoon might be playful. I forgot, or didn't take seriously enough, that they are also first-rate actors with devotion to craft. The kids this day were noisy and restless, but Mongezi would have none of it. He reprimanded the children early on, telling them to be quiet and pay attention. For the first time I saw them intimidated, even a little scared.

Mongezi told the children that each character in a play has a need and those needs come into conflict with the needs of other characters. If the actor knows his or her character's needs, then he or she will know the character's emotions at any point in the play. He then went around the room, interrogating each of the kids: What is your character? What is your character's most important line? What is your character feeling at that moment? Say the line. Say it again now, but properly.

It was a bit painful but also comic to watch my suddenly shy thespians. Some of them didn't give Mongezi much to work with. Munashe said her most important line was "Anon."

"What does that mean?" Mongezi asked her.

"I don't know."

"What are you feeling when you say 'Anon?'"

"Happy," she said.

"Why are you happy?"

"Because we are going to see Macbeth."

"Why are you happy to see Macbeth?"

She thought for a minute. "I don't know," she said.

I felt a huge inadequacy for what the children didn't know. Mongezi was tough, maybe too tough, but the children didn't wilt. They'd been through lots of storms in their lives. Mongezi was but a passing raincloud.

At the end of the afternoon they had earned his respect. We gathered in the large front room of the school and watched Mongezi and Xolani act out monologues from the *Mendi* play. Mongezi performed a riveting scene when he tells a young woman that she is now a widow after her husband has drowned in the sinking. He sat on the floor in front of us, perfectly still, dropping his head between his legs. We waited. And waited. I thought maybe he had fallen asleep. When he looked up, he had tears in his eyes. His voice was choked. His speech to the invisible widow was so real I thought maybe some of the kids believed a man *had* drowned. When he finished, they burst into applause.

I asked him how he did that—make himself cry.

"I am remembering something so sad it makes me cry," he said.

"Do you always remember the same thing?" I asked.

"Yes," he said.

"What is that?"

He paused.

"I am seeing a little boy getting run over by a truck."

"Oh," the children said.

At the end of our time together I wanted the children to also see the fun side of Mongezi, a wonderfully comical, physical actor. I asked him to reprise a funny scene from *Hungry Road* in which he plays a lion, but he deferred, coming up with his own solution.

"Do you want me to make you laugh?" he asked the kids.

"Yes!" they yelled.

He started laughing and laughing, getting louder and more maniacal. What's he doing, I wondered. He stopped.

"Can you do that?" The children mimicked him, laughing loud and long.

"There," he said. "I made you laugh."

After the groans died down, Nthabiseng, as usual speaking for the group, thanked Mongezi and Xolani for "taking time out of your day to come and see us, the children of fire." Then, as usual, she led the thank-you cheer, the group of kids ending with a rambunctious "*Ee-yoh, ee-yoh!*"

17

March 11: "I was Burnt in a Big, Big House"

THE KIDS WROTE HAIKU poems today. I wanted to give them a poetic structure in which to be creative. It was harder for them than I thought. Some had trouble counting syllables. They'd read a line and ask, "Is that five syllables?" They dawdled and dawdled. Some, like Lance, kept asking silly questions ("Where is that pencil I had last time?"). I said, "Lance, I bet I can write a haiku poem in the time that you come up with your next question." I wrote:

> *Lance Van Rooyen asks*
> *Way too many things of me*
> *He must keep working.*

Feleng, as usual, finished first and started reading a soccer magazine. I asked to see his work, expecting something shoddy and unfinished. He showed me this:

> *I was burnt in a*
> *Big, big house in Lesotho*
> *I was not happy.*

I asked him to read it out loud, and when he did, I praised him. I counted out the syllables, showing the others the five/seven/

five structure. I also said that Feleng's haiku expressed a simple but powerful thought. Could they do the same? They went back to work. But before the others even finished, Feleng showed me a *second* haiku:

> *In the hospital*
> *My family were crying*
> *I was left in hospital.*

When I showed this to Bronwen that afternoon, she said that was the case. Feleng's family visited him only once when he was in hospital and they cried. Then they left for a few years.

The haiku form pulled from Feleng something he might not otherwise have been able to express. And even though his second haiku was not quite five/seven/five, none of the other children could match the simple power of his two quickly-composed poems. In fact, few others composed a real haiku poem, instead stringing together unrelated lines. Nonetheless, their poems sometimes achieved striking effects.

> *I hate computers*
> *And I love my Mom and Dad*
> *I love to camp too.*
> —Nelson Tshabalala

> *I love my mother*
> *I'd like to be a doctor*
> *I miss Nhlanhla.*
> —Nthabiseng Nkashe

> *I am Zulu girl*
> *I like Anele because*
> *She is a good friend.*
> —Munashe Anderson

> *I am a Sotho*
> *I love people in the world*

I went to London.
—Dikeledi Mboko

Zanele is quiet
Nthabiseng has a leg
Children of Fire.
—Dikeledi Mboko

Watched Macbeth Friday
I killed Lady Macduff's kid
I killed Duncan's kids.
—Lance Van Rooyen

For anyone but Lance, this haiku might signal some emotional trauma. But knowing his delight in the macabre, I thought: "That's just Lance being Lance."

Lance Van Rooyen

Portrait: Feleng Lebaka

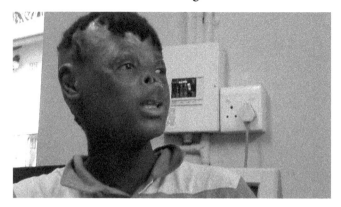

Feleng Lebaka

If there is a poster child for Children of Fire, it is Feleng. The website has more than 120 pictures of Feleng, far more than any other child. (Nelson is next among the Macbethers with thirty-two.) Feleng is also the longest current resident other than Dorah, having arrived at age three.

Feleng was burned terribly in a shack fire at the age of one month. Among other injuries, he lost much of his forehead in the fire. The gaping hole in his skull was exacerbated by sepsis after the injury. As with Dorah, Bronwen has gone to great lengths to get Feleng first-rate medical care.

In August 2008, Bronwen took Feleng, then age six, in the first of two trips to Zurich, Switzerland, where surgeons and professors at University Hospital determined the best way to reconstruct his skull. Bronwen engaged the interest of a reporter from Zurich's daily German-language newspaper, *Tages Anzeiger (Daily Gazette)*, who then wrote a lengthy feature story titled "Der Kleine Feleng hofft auf Hilfe in Zurich" ("Little Feleng hopes to get help in Zurich."). Bronwen asked that the story be written as a way of putting pressure on surgeons so they would have no choice but to operate for free. It worked.

Seven months later, Feleng made a second trip to Switzerland. The South African newspaper *The Citizen* headlined its story:

"Burn Boy Jets Off to Europe in Search of a New Face." By now Feleng had also become a celebrity in Zurich where he'd been "adopted" during his visits by a Swiss woman, Kari Sulc, and where readers knew of the burned boy from South Africa who loved to take pictures.

In surgery several of Feleng's ribs were extracted and inserted into his skull to cover the hole at the top of his forehead. Feleng's ongoing medical needs are "huge," Bronwen says. "Feleng needs a nose grown from his arm (tagliocozzi), [and] latissimus dorsi lifted from his back and put on the back of his head," she wrote in an email. "He needs digital distraction."

I had to look up Bronwen's medical terms. "Tagliocozzi" refers to a method developed by Gaspare Tagliacozzi (1547–1599), an Italian plastic surgeon, for replacing a missing nose with skin from the patient's upper arm. "Digital distraction"—also called distraction osteogenesis or osteodistraction—is a procedure used to reconstruct skeletal deformities or lengthen the long bones of the body. A bone is fractured into two segments which are gradually moved apart during the distraction phase, allowing new bone to form in the gap. Feleng needs this procedure for his right hand.

Feleng and Bronwen have a complicated but loving relationship. Since an early age he has had to deal not only with repeated surgeries, but lack of a family.

"They've entirely abandoned him," Bronwen said. "All the other children in that family are in care. They were all dumped." Bronwen said Feleng's mother struggled with alcohol addiction and Feleng's father was said to have taken his own life after Feleng got burned.

Feleng knows the realities of which Bronwen speaks. He, Dorah, Sizwe, and Dikeledi have no parents or have parents who abandoned them. Of those four, Bronwen has adopted Dorah and Sizwe. She hopes someone will adopt Dikeledi.

Feleng is now under the foster care supervision of Mitta Lebaka, a child burn survivor and Children of Fire social worker with whom Feleng has formed a close attachment. Mitta and Feleng are both ethnically Sotho. She's helped him connect with his Sotho roots by taking him to Lesotho, the "mountain kingdom" nation located inside South Africa. He uses her surname and calls himself Feleng Lebaka. It's not his legal name, Bronwen says, "only in his heart."

18

The Emotional Health of Child Burn Survivors

THE EMOTIONAL HEALTH OF the children I worked with belies the trauma many of them experienced and that some continue to experience. As Bronwen and a colleague wrote on the Children of Fire website, the emotional strain for a child burn survivor begins right away with the burn injury:

> When a child is admitted to hospital with burns, she is suddenly separated from her familiar environment and placed in a strange, frightening place, where her parents are no longer in control and where strangers are hurting her. The burned patient is usually fully conscious at the time of admission, unlike patients with other severe trauma . . . The burned child feels shock, fear, bewilderment, and intense pain.[1]

In the longer term, many burned children experience anxiety, depression, grief, and post-traumatic stress symptoms such as re-experiencing the event in recollections or nightmares.[2] According to one study, a child's emotional response to burns varies according

1. Jones and Bloomberg, "Psychological Problems after Burns," para. 2.

2. Armstrong et al., "Acute Reactions," 65, and Brown et al., "Inpatient Consultation and Liaison," 136.

to the age at which they suffered injury. Before the age of eighteen months, children generally "incorporate the burn into their own body image," as seemed to be the case with several children of fire.[3] School-age children like Clara, age eight when she was injured, "recognize the change and grieve the loss." Adolescents generally "respond with anger, guilt and anxiety."[4] (This seemed not to be the case with Munashe, who was twelve when burned, but perhaps I don't know her full story.)

Recent research has highlighted a hopeful psychological prognosis for child burn survivors. While earlier studies reported that most burned children demonstrated serious adjustment problems (up to 80 percent), more recent studies show much lower rates of child psychopathology on the order of 15 to 20 percent.[5] And while it is true that burned children in both younger (ages four to eleven) and older (ages twelve to eighteen) groups showed higher rates than other children for anxiety, depression, sleep problems, and attention deficit, the group mean for these children was still within the normal range.[6] Recent research also indicates these findings:

- The size of the burn in total body surface area (TBSA) does not affect long-term psychological well-being (one study even showed that children with more severe burns were more socially competent);

- The visibility of the burn injury does not affect long-term psychological well-being;

- Greater time since burn injury increases the likelihood of psychosocial adjustment;

- Length of hospitalization does not affect the child's psychological well-being;

3. Armstrong et al., "Acute Reactions," 66.
4. Ibid., 66.
5. Tarnowski and Rasnake, "Long–term Psychosocial Sequelae," 108.
6. See Blakeney et al., "Familial Values as Factors," 472–75.

- Overall, child burn survivors generally have few problems with self-esteem.[7]

In short, children of fire have every chance of adjusting socially and psychologically to their circumstances. One report concludes that although children and adolescent burn survivors may be more at risk for anxiety or depressive disorders, most appear to have the resources for eventually coping with their injury and its aftermath.[8]

One huge caveat is in order, though. Almost *all* of the pediatric burn research in English focuses on American or British children. These children generally come from intact nuclear families with access to a full range of health professionals: surgeons, nurses, social workers, physical therapists, occupational therapists and the like. Children who show the most positive adjustment to their burn injuries come from families characterized by "adequate resources, social support networks, cohesiveness, and effective communication and conflict resolution."[9] Such families self-report marital integrity, an atmosphere of open discussion, and family participation in cultural and recreational activities.[10] By contrast, some of our Macbethers do not even *have* a family. Their parents are deceased or unable to cope with their own lives, much less that of a severely burned child. Children of Fire is the child's family, with Bronwen—"Mama"—the mother.

In South Africa, psychological support for child burn patients is limited at best. Bronwen told me that counseling

> rarely achieves what we need because experienced counselors who are actually prepared to give their time have mostly been white and Anglo and have too narrow a frame of reference to relate to the cultural and linguistic backgrounds of our children. You have to live alongside and in and with disability and disfigurement to know what it *feels* like.

7. Tarnowski and Rasnake, "Long–term Psychosocial Sequelae," 106, 111.

8. Armstrong et al., "Acute Reactions," 64.

9. Tarnowski and Brown, "Future Directions," 272. See also, Blakeney et al., "Familial Values as Factors," 475.

10. Bush and Maron, "Pain Management," 158.

Bronwen lives with the children and knows something of their languages and cultures. She's written dual-language African children's books and so has learned traditional customs and has a basic knowledge of Sotho and Zulu.

Bronwen is hopeful but honest about how much can be done for a child's emotional well-being. "No one person, nor one approach, has all the answers," she said, going on to explain:

> Often we take one step forward and two steps back. We do a lot with a group approach. Like a mini-Parliament, we gather in the garden to debate the problem of the day—who is surly, who is stealing, who is sad, and why, and how we can ease the problem. I have always loved the wisdom, the clarity, of children. They cut to the chase far more quickly, far more effectively, than adults. But not every problem can be fixed. Every child is different and each one of them presents a different challenge. The issues they have when they are three years old are very different when they start school, even more perilous when they start high school, oh-so-difficult when they start becoming attracted to the opposite sex, and so cruel when they start looking for work. At each stage they need an emotional punching bag, a buttress, someone who, when the shouting is done, is still there with a hug, come what may. It's an unending story. Life itself is the therapy—life and love.

19

March 15: "Fire Burn and Cauldron Bubble!"

YESTERDAY WAS QUITE A day: the group's public performance of *Macbeth*. The stage was the Children of Fire house lawn and the audience was twenty-two American students and their professors from Penn State University. To our Macbethers it might as well have been Broadway, for all their nervous excitement. The Americans had come over from the guesthouse where they—and I—were staying. When Bronwen found out that a group of American students was staying nearby, she took the children to meet them, showing up one evening unannounced with six or seven kids and adorable baby Rien. The children worked their magic on the Americans, singing and laughing and telling stories. From there it was easy to get the Penn Staters to be the children's first (and only) *Macbeth* audience.

When I went to fetch the kids at school for the performance, they were manic with excitement. After we walked down to the "theater"—kiddy chairs arranged in a semicircle on the house lawn—the children fetched the props: three witches' black robes, two swords (one of them a long stick), the rubbish bin cauldron, and Bronwen's stuffed fox as Graymalkin the cat.

In our short, chaotic, pre-performance rehearsal, I couldn't get the children's attention. Nthabiseng and Munashe battled each other with swords while Feleng literally tied himself in knots inside his black witch's robe. Lance kept asking if he could play Macduff, even though his ride would be coming at any moment. And Nelson, our cool comedian, was panicked with performance anxiety though he had only a tiny role as the messenger Ross.

Given the chaos, I decided to work with two characters at a time. I looked at the time—4:36. Soon I would fetch the Penn Staters for our 5:30 show time, yet my cast had not yet run through most of their performance. What they *had* done was gamely choreographed a death scene in which Macbeth (Nthabiseng), fencing on one leg, spears Munashe (Young Siward) who collapses to the ground. Nelson runs in from offstage and counts her out like a boxer knocked to the canvas. The Scottish play was turning from tragedy to farce.

Nthabiseng (Macbeth) and Munashe (Young Siward)

Shortly after 5:00 p.m. we heard two women's screams coming from Sunbury Avenue, just over the back wall. The kids ran (or in Nthabiseng's case, hopped) up a flight of stairs to a rooftop balcony overlooking the street. I tried to stop them, saying we had only ten minutes left of rehearsal time. Those who went up yelled something to those who stayed behind.

"What? A gun?" Anele said, standing next to me.

"What are they saying?" I asked.

"They say that two women were being chased by a man with a gun," she said.

Now *I* ran up the stairs, and the rest followed. Nthabiseng was yelling down to the street to two sharply dressed young black women. They looked shaken. One was on her cell phone. Nthabiseng asked if they were all right and if there was anything we could do, like call the police. They said no, and soon they were let through the front gate of a house where they'd been standing.

We went back to rehearsal, but the kids had lost focus. Of all the storied mishaps during productions of *Macbeth*, this might have been the only time a rehearsal had been interrupted by an attempted mugging. I later told Bronwen what happened, and she said that Sunbury Avenue was more dangerous than other streets because it lacked the tiny security kiosks with guards that could be found on other streets. I mentioned how maturely Nthabiseng reacted.

"Our children have responded to various muggings," Bronwen said matter-of-factly. "They've even stopped a few."

When I went to fetch the Penn Staters, I saw Loide leading them down the street like the Pied Piper: she'd walked to the guesthouse and gotten them herself. As the Penn Staters found their seats in the kiddy chairs, a noisy squabble broke out backstage—that is, behind the bush that shielded the actors from view. I went back to break it up and told the kids to go out and introduce themselves by name, age, hometown, and roles. Another squabble. Who would go first? I grabbed Lance and shoved him out front. The Penn Staters applauded enthusiastically to every introduction—expecting, I feared, a show that would be just as good.

Act I, Scene I, all forty-five seconds of it, went off without a hitch. It began with Bronwen shaking a large sheet of plastic to make the sound of thunder, as she told the children had been done in Shakespeare's day (though not with plastic). The three witches gathered around the rubbish bin cauldron: Lance in a sweatshirt and jeans, Feleng in the black cape which he flourished dramatically, and Munashe in her flaming orange-and-black top with a maroon stocking cap over her tissue expander, incongruously carrying a sword which she would later use as Young Siward.

The witches: Lance, Feleng, Munashe

The witches spoke their lines sharply and well, each of them lifting their arms skyward as they spoke, invoking a power from beyond. They concluded with the chant, "Fair is foul, and foul is fair: Hover through the fog and filthy air," circling the cauldron as they had rehearsed so many times. The Penn Staters broke into applause. I then announced we would skip over the rest of the play until the last scene, which drew a big laugh.

Nthabiseng, clad in Viking helmet, red jersey and skirt, and with her crutch under the arm that held her sword, stepped out and read Macbeth's soliloquy: "They have tied me to a stake; I cannot fly, / But bearlike I must fight the course. What's he / That was not born of woman? Such a one / Am I to fear, or none."

Munashe, still dressed as Witch 3 but now playing Young Siward, entered with sword in hand and challenged Macbeth: "Thou liest, abhorred tyrant; with my sword / I'll prove the lie thou speak'st."

She said it well, but apparently not well enough for her high standards. As we waited eagerly for her to engage Macbeth in swordplay, she repeated her line three times, stopping at one point to laugh at her mispronunciation of "abhorred." Nthabiseng, with sword upraised, stood by patiently.

Munashe and Nthabiseng fought skillfully and well, not surprising given they'd spent most of rehearsal time practicing! Macbeth found an opening in Young Siward's mid-section and thrust the sword in. Munashe fell back dramatically, clearly dead. Nelson, and now Lance and Anele, jumped out from the bush, counted her out, and carted her off. Everyone laughed—including Macbeth!

Then Macbeth and Macduff (Dikeledi) gave brief soliloquies, followed by the off-stage cast making "Alarum" sounds, as per stage direction: "*Woooooooo—eeeeeeeee—whooooo—eeeeeeeeee.*"

Siward (Feleng in black cape) and Malcolm (Zanele), son of the slain King Duncan, entered stage left, with Siward shoving the heir apparent to keep her moving. After a brief dialogue about the favorable turn of events in the war against Macbeth, they retired to the grey plastic castle in the children's sandbox, ducking to enter only to reappear giant-like above the parapets, again drawing a huge laugh.

Feleng (Siward) and Zanele (Malcolm) at the castle

Next came the dramatic finale between Macbeth and Macduff. Unfortunately, just as Macduff (Dikeledi) challenged Macbeth—"Turn, hell-hound, turn!"—she realized she had no sword to fight, having left it offstage. Macbeth waited while her sworn enemy fetched her weapon. They fought, and exited fighting.

The rest of the play fell apart after that. When Siward (Feleng) was supposed to learn from Ross (Nelson) of Young Siward's brave death at the hand of Macbeth, each boy froze. The other children yelled from offstage: "Feleng! Nelson!"

Feleng looked especially confused, at one point sitting down and laughing while we waited for him to speak his lines. By the time Macduff (Dikeledi) entered with Macbeth's severed (doll's) head, the play almost grinded to a halt. But Anele saved the day. She made the most of her tiny nonspeaking part by majestically entering with the Viking helmet to crown Malcolm (Zanele) as the new king.

While the Penn Staters applauded, thinking the performance was over, the cast assembled for the *piece de resistance*. Feleng fetched the African drum (which he promptly dropped—*thud!*) and the eight Macbethers lined up in front of the audience.

"Since we skipped about 97 percent of the play," I announced, "we thought we'd summarize it with a rap." The Penn Staters cheered. (I'd written the rap earlier with the children, realizing almost too late how little of the play they actually knew.)

Nelson leaned over the drum and got us going with a lively beat. I chanted the rap on the verses, but the kids got down on the refrain, growing louder and louder and dancing as Nelson accompanied them.

Fair is foul and foul is fair
Hover through the fog and filthy air
Talkin' to Macbeth, givin' him a thrill
"You can be King—you just gotta kill!"

Double, double, toil and trouble,
Fire burn and cauldron bubble!

Glam's and Cawdor and King hereafter.
Careful Macbeth— gonna be a disaster!

Double, double, toil and trouble,
Fire burn and cauldron bubble!

Making a stew with guts and blood
Boil it all down till the charm is good
Telling Macbeth not to worry a thing
No man of woman born can kill you as king.

Double, double, toil and trouble,
Fire burn and cauldron bubble!

Macdonwald, Duncan, MacDuff's son
Macbeth kill 'em all before the play is done.
But taking them all is not quite enough,
Cuz in the end you gotta face MacDuff!
OOH man—you lost your head!
"Sorry Macbeth, but you're really quite dead."

Fair is foul and foul is fair
Hover through the fog and filthy air

Double, double, toil and trouble,
Fire burn and cauldron bubble!(2x)

The kids loved the line "Sorry Macbeth, but you're really quite dead." They'd walk around shaking their heads and looking at the ground in fateful resignation over Macbeth's grim beheading.

Doing the *Macbeth* rap: Lance, Feleng, Nthabiseng, Anele, Nelson (on drum), Zanele, Dikeledi, the author

When the rap ended, the Penn Staters burst into applause. The kids bowed modestly—all except Feleng, who stepped out and bowed grandly with a broad sweep of his cape.

Nthabiseng then called Bronwen down to the stage and gave her as a present the book *Will in the World* by Stephen Greenblatt, which I'd bought for the occasion. Surprised but composed, and holding Rien in her arms, Bronwen told the Penn Staters: "Some of you are going to *have* to volunteer now so I can have time to read this."

Then the children pulled another surprise. They had been asked to sing "Happy Birthday" to Holly, the Penn State faculty leader. They did far more than that: they *choreographed* the song with pairs of kids entering from different directions, each singing a verse in a different style and rhythm. They then presented Holly with two birthday cards they'd made, expressing surprising affection for a woman they'd just met. Then they sang three *more* verses of "Happy Birthday": "We wish you many more," "May God bless you," and ending with "How old are you now?" She replied that she was thirty-five, so the kids, led by Nthabiseng, rhythmically clapped and counted in unison to thirty-five as everyone laughed. "She'll be thirty-six by the time you guys finish!" I joked.

Having the stage, the children then *held* it, singing a medley of pop, Christian, and African songs. They asked the Penn Staters to honor them with a song, which the Americans did with "I'll Make a Man Out of You" from *Mulan*, the Disney film from their childhood. The Macbethers clapped and hooted. Bronwen had ordered twenty pizzas to share but the Penn State group had time for only a slice before heading out to celebrate Holly's birthday.

I stayed and ate pizza. Bronwen (holding Rien at times) and I shared a bottle of red wine while the children ran about the yard. It was my first chance to see Mama *be* Mama for any length of time. Usually I just saw her around the office. Now she was in full Mama mode, giving orders ("Anele, hold Rien's head *up!*" "Feleng, get the cups on the counter." "Dikeledi, run into the house and get a cloth to take care of that spill."), but also telling stories in a way that captured the children's attention. Her criticism and occasional sarcasm had the soft edge of love. When the kids broke into a game of hide-and-seek, she simply could not abide the way they played. She told them they shouldn't make noise as they ran off to hide. She also didn't like it that the kids tried to make it back to home base before being caught. To her mind, all of the hiders must be found by the seeker. "That's why it's called hide and *seek*," she said.

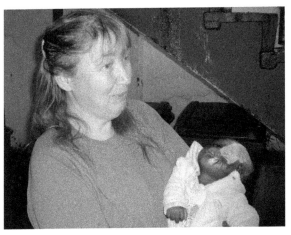

Bronwen Jones and Rien ne Dit

As the evening darkened and the children went off to bed, Bronwen rocked Rien, his one good eye fixed upon her. She was at peace. I felt at peace. I walked back to the guesthouse as the stars came out over Johannesburg. It had been a good night.

The next day Bronwen wrote me this email: "Feleng says he did badly because he used your edition of *Macbeth* and the writing was smaller or layout different to the book he was used to. He only sees with one eye."

Portrait: Bronwen Jones

It's not easy to get information from Bronwen Jones about herself. It's not that she's secretive about her life. She just doesn't think it's important in the larger scheme of things. When I asked her to tell me about herself she said, "There's an article on the website with some bio stuff."

I went to the website and learned things about her that she had not shared in her office. She grew up in England but is fiercely Welsh. Her grandfather, Thomas Jones (1870–1955), was a Welsh civil servant who advised four British prime ministers from 1916 to 1930. He was so often consulted on Welsh political matters that he came to be known as the unofficial Secretary of State for Wales. Her father Tristan, for whom her son is named, was manager of *The Observer* newspaper in London.

Bronwen is my age, born in 1957. As a child, she once took baby foxes to school in her blazer pocket. She was proficient at piano, viola, and harp. When she was told at age ten that she had to be eleven to join the school orchestra, she started her own orchestra. As a young woman she worked as a barmaid and as a walking billboard. Later she taught English to the Turkish military and edited newspapers. She is a qualified engineering geologist who wrote and edited magazine articles on tunnels. She even co-wrote a book on The Chunnel (*The Tunnel: Channel and Beyond*, 1987).

More than twenty years ago Bronwen came to South Africa with her ex-husband, a journalist, expecting to stay a few years. From the start she committed herself to working for social justice. In 1991, five Afrikaner men in their twenties chased down three black men at a dam near Groblersdal, 120 kilometers (75 miles) northeast of Pretoria, shooting and killing two of them. A third escaped. Bronwen befriended that man, Rickson Shirinda, offering him space in their tiny two-room flat along with her husband, herself, their ten-month-old son Tristan, and a little African girl they were caring for, Thobe.

Shortly after that she met Norman Ntswane, the brother of one of the murdered men, Lloyd Ntswane. Together Norman and

Bronwen drove far and wide looking for evidence of the murder. With their help, the men were convicted. Two years later Norman's daughter, Wendy, was born. Wendy Ntswane is the Wendy who volunteers at Children of Fire.

After writing children's books for several years, Bronwen learned about Dorah, saved her from having her eyes excised, and took her in. "And that was that," Bronwen said, "because Dorah became time-consuming." Bronwen's writing career ended, as did her marriage. She had not expected to lead a charity, and now it is her life. She works fifteen hours a day, seven days a week, and responds to emails as late as midnight. She knows all of the children of fire as if they are her own kids—which, in fact, some are.

Children of Fire runs on a shoestring budget funded by private donors and on Bronwen's ability to coax free surgeries from physicians and gifts from corporate sponsors. She is known as Mama Mahala—*mahala* means free in the Sotho language.

"All this pulling the heart-strings or pressurizing people is actually draining," she said. "It's like a stage performance, and though I'm not on stage I still can't do them every day."

She no longer takes a salary after receiving a stipend from a corporation the first few years.

For her efforts there is now a great difference between the children of fire, who "are going on with their lives and may do great things," and the thousands of child burn survivors throughout Africa who are marginalized or forgotten.

Children of Fire is more than a home and school. In 2001, Bronwen helped organize the UMashesha volunteers, a group that responds to fires in the townships. UMashesha means "quick helper or mover" in all of the Nguni languages, such as Zulu and Xhosa. The volunteers are community safety workers from informal settlements who are trained in fire prevention, firefighting, hazmat, and first aid. They make safety presentations in schools and community centers and offer firefighting courses and first aid training. They also place large firefighting water tanks in crowded settlements where water is most needed and fire engines cannot go. (The water in the tanks is dyed green to discourage people from using it for cooking and washing.) Such water tanks "have saved a significant number of lives," Bronwen said. After a fire in a township or squatter camp, UMashesha volunteers provide disaster recovery bags to those whose homes were burned. The sturdy red cotton bags are made by a women's cooperative and contain provisions for a few days: first aid supplies, nonperishable food, saucepans, sugar cane gel stoves, safety candle holders, crockery, cutlery, washing materials, books and pens for children to take to school, outfits of second hand clothes, and shoes.

An engineer by training, Bronwen hopes to create safer home environments through advances in product design. "As long as people have illegal electricity wired in a dodgy way, or have a candle for light, or cheaply made paraffin stoves which explode pretty much when you first light them because it's such crappy metal—all those different things—they will carry on having devastating injuries," she told me. "We need to keep thinking out of the box to find new ways to tackle the problem."

She talks with inventors about stoves, heaters, and candle holders that can be made safe and affordable for the poorest of the poor. She is also pushing for a ban on a particularly unsafe cooking stove which leaks paraffin. She hopes to introduce small solar heaters into squatter camps because solar power is affordable and safe.

Beyond South Africa, Bronwen has established Children of Fire connections in Tunisia and the Democratic Republic of the Congo (DRC), though neither of these requires a large outlay of money. In Tunis, Children of Fire supports surgery and burn rehabilitation at Ben Arous Hospital. In the DRC, Bronwen organized doctors from South Africa, the United States, and Italy to perform fifty-seven operations in December 2013.

From Bronwen's own experience she knows that not all children are burned unintentionally: some are set on fire. Her adopted son, Sizwe, born in 2001 in Kwazulu Natal, was allegedly burned by his mother (his father is not known). He was taken from his mother and placed in a home for AIDS orphans because it was the safest place that could be found. When Sizwe arrived at Children of Fire most of his hair was missing and his left hand and arm were badly burned. His left ear was also missing. Eyelid contractures meant he had to sleep with his eyes partially opened. After multiple surgeries, Sizwe now lives with Bronwen, Tristan, and Dorah, shuttling between Johannesburg and London for additional surgeries.

While a source estimates that 10 to 25 percent of pediatric burn injuries are deliberately inflicted by adults, Bronwen puts the rate at 30 percent in Africa—and in England too.[1] Intentional burns, which occur most often in infants and toddlers, are hugely underreported, she says. Even at a conservative estimate, it's possible that more than 10,000 children worldwide die each year from being intentionally scalded or set on fire. About 30 percent of children who are set on fire die, compared to 2 percent of children with accidental burn injuries.[2]

"A big part of the problem is that people are embarrassed to seek help when they face a nervous breakdown, so they take out their anger or fear on the weakest around them: they set their nearest and dearest alight," Bronwen said. "There are far too many children being born that can't be looked after because people don't want them."

She told me that if she were to start over again she would work on issues of family planning and birth control. "There are four million people in squatter camps [in South Africa], many without access to food, water, and safe power—and many children without opportunity or hope," she said. "There are just too many people."

In 2015, Bronwen Jones received the British Empire Medal for Services to Young People.

Bronwen can't imagine the turn her life took in any other way.

"Once you look burn kids in the eyes and know that you can improve their lives," she said, "you can't *not* go to help them."

---

1. Purdue et al., "Child Abuse by Burning," 221.
2. Brown et al., "Inpatient," 124.

20

"What Children of Fire Means to Me"

Writing class: Anele, Munashe, Dikeledi, Lance, Nelson

Anele

Children of Fire means a lot to me because it is a wonderful charity and it helped a lot with my operations now i am feeling better and also here you travel the holl wourld you go wach moveis, and visit people . . . here is like my home and i would like to say thanks to mama for everything that she have doen for us. And when i go home i will miss [ran out of time]

Feleng

Children of Fire has helped me a lot when it mean I have had so many thing. It has helped me to be what I want to be I came here when I was three years old in 2003 I was happy to come here in children of I had people around me I was happy I like Brown Jones, and Sizwe Jones, Tristan Jones, and Dorah Jones. They were kind to me. Than in Children of Fire Brown Jone took me over to sea, to Switzerland for surgery. The person who was looking after me her name was Kari whe we got to her house I had banana bried for a sank. I came back to South Africa I came back people were happy to see me Bronwan was so glad to see me.

Nthabiseng

Children of Fire mean a lots stuff to, like Children of Fire help me a lot oparetions, and Children of Fire show me a lots place that even I didn't know I will ever see them. I would like to thanks Mama Jones to having a wounderful love. Now Children of Fire has help me to understand my sutuation and to understand my life Children of Fire is so brave as brave as lion as sweet as sugar cane as cool as cucumber. And I don't like people calling us/starring at us keep on @ shame on us. And the day I will go home I will never forget that I did get help from Children of Fire. Children is a wise Solom[on]. I love you.

Nelson

Children of Fire means a lot to me because they have helped me from 2009. My hands were like [crossed out word]. My knuckles both of my hands were like that then I came to children of fire then they took me to hospital. Then they amputated one of my fingers so then Mama made a t-shurt wich is reten Do not Amputate Without Permission!!! Then he did not amputate from that day. Then they operated my right hand i like went to hospital. So in 2010 they operated me 10 times so my hands look better then they look know. So children of Fire is the best because they help. And even know we are going to hospital. GOOD BYE PEOPLE

Zanele

Children of Fire means a lot they helped me with my operation, I've been at the places which I never been. And some times I feel happy know. I feel better even when I have some scares. And I have more friends. And they are very kind to me. And I love them.

Note: These were the children present this day.

21

March 16: "They Shall be Comforted"

Yesterday I drove Anele, Munashe, Clara, and Perlucia to Chris Hani Baragwanath Hospital in Soweto to see Hlumelo who was recovering from surgery on his arm. Bronwen gave me a parcel of two peaches, an apple, a plum, and an orange.

"Don't they feed him?" I asked.

"Not what he should eat," she said.

I told her I wasn't sure I could find my way.

"The girls will tell you," she said.

They did. Anele and Munashe sat with me in the front, Clara and Perlucia in the back. Occasionally I'd feel a touch on my shoulder or neck, like the brush of an insect or a falling leaf. It was Perlucia pulling herself up to get a better view. At one point I turned to look over my shoulder at traffic. About six inches from my face there she was, quietly looking up at me.

Anele and Munashe occasionally argued about directions, but I knew to prefer Anele. Munashe tends to blurt things out without thinking, plus she struggles with getting the right words in English. She would say "Go here" or "Go this way" and I'd have to see which way she was pointing. Anele playfully chastised her for not knowing right from left. At one point as we approached a traffic circle, Munashe said, "Go around this thingy then go there." That broke everyone up, even the little ones.

Munashe kept up a running commentary on just about everything she saw, including hundreds of Kaizer Chief and Orlando Pirate supporters blowing vuvuzelas and singing on their way to the big derby at FNB Stadium.

I was worried we'd get stuck in traffic, but Anele steered us well, avoiding a jammed off-ramp by finding the way to the hospital from the next exit. Today was Anele's birthday (fourteen) and Clara's (ten). When we arrived at Bara, four or five nurses let out a small cheer and greeted Munashe and Anele so warmly it seemed as if they were meeting old friends, which was more or less the case, given all the time the girls had spent on the surgery ward.

A girl who had attended Beka School last year was sitting up in one of the twenty beds lined up in two rows of ten. While Munashe and Anele chatted with her, Clara, Perlucia, and I marched off to find Hlumelo in one of the three other children's wards.

The hallways seemed to be abandoned. Doors were open to every room—staff toilets, meeting rooms, medical supply rooms. I could have walked into any of them. Theft, however, was discouraged, at least in part, by security checks of cars entering and leaving the hospital grounds.

I looked for Hlumelo. I entered one of the wards. Was he here? Family members were visiting children at most bedsides. The kids' injuries looked typical: broken bones and partial body casts, but no burn victims other than Hlumelo, wherever he was.

When Munashe and Anele entered they walked directly to Hlumelo's bed, not far from where I'd been standing. I hadn't recognized him! He was sleeping, his back turned to us and shirtless in the warm room. He was wearing green-and-beige-striped pajama bottoms with "BARA" written down the side. One hand was in a cast up to the elbow.

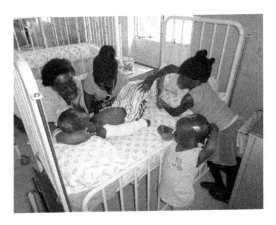

Hlumelo visited by Anele, Munashe, Perlucia, and Clara

He looked so peaceful I wondered if we should disturb him. Anele gently nudged him awake. He looked up, saw us, and then sat up, not saying a word.

I asked him if he wanted an orange. He nodded yes. I peeled the orange and fed him slice by slice. He ate slowly but steadily.

I took out the book I bought for him that morning: *Curious George Goes to the Toy Factory*. I read animatedly, but he seemed distracted, looking off occasionally to see what was going on around him. The other four children enjoyed the story more than he.

"Wow, I really gave that my best shot," I whispered to Anele. "Is he too tired to listen?"

"He doesn't understand English," she said.

I had no idea! Hlumelo and I had been buddies for six weeks, greeting each other every day. But thinking back I realized I never actually *said* anything to him other than hi and bye.

"What's his language?" I asked.

Xhosa, they told me.

"Who speaks Xhosa?"

"I speak Xhosa," Clara said confidently. "Give the book to me."

"Hai Clara! You do not speak Xhosa!" Anele admonished her. Munashe and Clara, from Zimbabwe, speak Shona. Anele speaks Xhosa. Perlucia, whatever her language, does not yet read.

I gave Anele the book. She translated the story for Hlumelo. This time he was riveted. Anele read and pointed to pictures of George being scolded by the store manager for sneaking in and climbing to the top shelf of toys but then, as always, saving the day by handing toys down to children as they asked for them. The store manager made a bundle on sales and George was elevated from petty thief to assistant store manager.

Anele reads to Hlumelo

When Anele finished, Hlumelo said something quietly to her and lay back down.

"Does he want to go back to sleep?" I asked. We'd been there only ten minutes.

"No, he is hungry."

"Oh, does he want another piece of fruit?"

She leaned in and whispered to him. He nodded yes.

I looked at the four remaining fruits: apple, plum, two peaches. But how could he eat any of these? With a fully bandaged hand and limited use of fingers on the other hand he could not hold food. Munashe gave him a plum, but it fell from his arms onto the bed sheet.

"No, Munashe!" Anele scolded.

"We need a knife," I said. "If we had a knife we could cut this into pieces and feed him."

Of course they didn't have a knife sitting out in the children's ward. So I stood behind Hlumelo—not that it would matter if he saw me—and bit into the plum. I took a small piece from my mouth, reached around, and put it into his mouth as he opened it. Munashe laughed, but no one else did, and in any case Hlumelo didn't know.

After he finished he lay back down. Anele leaned over and put her hand behind his head. Munashe leaned over too. Perlucia wanted to get up on the other side of the bed so I lifted her next to her little buddy. Clara also climbed up. I took a picture of the four of them surrounding their friend with comfort and love. The nurses rang the bell. Four o'clock. Visiting hours were over.

Munashe and Anele pulled up the bars on the sides of Hlumelo's bed. I put my hand on his bald head and told him we came because we were his friends and we cared. I asked if he understood and he nodded. Anele told him matter-of-factly that someone would come by on Monday. We said goodbye and walked off. Hlumelo turned his body toward us as we walked away. I looked back. He raised his good arm and waved, then resumed the fetal position we'd found him in.

On the way out the girls said goodbye to their friend in the first ward. She was taking a short walk back to her bed, helped by her mother. Only then did I see what I hadn't before: she was blind. Bronwen later told me that the young woman was not only blind, but had a brain tumor and was HIV-positive. She left the Johannesburg School for the Blind last year when she turned nineteen. "She was very far behind in her education," Bronwen said, "but we referred her on to vocational training."

I thought back to that Sunday when I first met the children of fire in church. Reverend Williams had said the Sermon on the Mount is about community. When those who mourn shall be comforted, the comfort doesn't come out of the heavens from an angel, or like a bolt of lightning. It comes from us. This day, and every day, the children showed me how.

Bibliography

Albertyn, Rene, et al. "Pediatric Burn Injuries in Sub-Saharan Africa—An Overview." *Burns* 32 (2006) 605–12.

American Society of Plastic Surgeons. "Tissue Expansion: Growing Extra Skin for Reconstruction." www.plasticsurgery.org/reconstructive-procedures/tissue-expansion.

Armstrong, F. Daniel, et al. "Acute Reactions." In *Behavioral Aspects of Pediatric Burns*, edited by Kenneth Tarnowski, 55–79. Issues in Clinical Child Psychology. Boston: Springer, 1994.

Blakeney, Patricia, et al. "Familial Values as Factors Influencing Long-term Psychological Adjustment of Children After Severe Burn Injury." *Journal of Burn Care and Rehabilitation* 11.5 (1990) 472–75.

Brown, Ronald T., et al. "Inpatient Consultation and Liaison." In *Behavioral Aspects of Pediatric Burns*, edited by Kenneth Tarnowski, 119–46. Issues in Clinical Child Psychology. Boston: Springer, 1994.

Bush, Joseph P., and Marlene T. Maron. "Pain Management." In *Behavioral Aspects of Pediatric Burns*, edited by Kenneth Tarnowski, 147–68. Issues in Clinical Child Psychology. Boston: Springer, 1994.

Jones, Bronwen, and Charissa Bloomberg. "Psychological Problems after Burns." http://www.childrenoffire.org/burnpsych.pdf.

Parbhoo, Asha, et al. "Burn Prevention Programs for Children in Developing Countries Require Urgent Attention: A Targeted Literature Review." *Burns* 36.2 (2010) 164–75.

Purdue, Gary F., et al., "Child Abuse by Burning—An Index of Suspicion." *The Journal of Trauma* 28.2 (1988) 221–24.

Schwebel, David, et al. "Paraffin-related Injuries in Low-income South African Communities: Knowledge, Practice and Perceived Risk." *Bulletin of the World Health Organization* 87.9 (2009) 700–6.

Tarnowski, Kenneth, ed. *Behavioral Aspects of Pediatric Burns*. Issues in Clinical Child Psychology. Boston: Springer, 1994.

Tarnowski, Kenneth, and Ronald T. Brown. "Future Directions." In *Behavioral Aspects of Pediatric Burns,* edited by Kenneth Tarnowski, 265–76. Issues in Clinical Child Psychology. Boston: Springer, 1994.

Tarnowski, Kenneth, and L. Kaye Rasnake. "Long–term Psychosocial Sequelae." In *Behavioral Aspects of Pediatric Burns,* edited by Kenneth Tarnowski, 81–118. Issues in Clinical Child Psychology. Boston: Springer, 1994.

Teo, Alison, et al. "A Comparison of the Epidemiology of Pediatric Burns in Scotland and South Africa." *Burns* 38 (2012) 802–6.

"Tissue Expanders." http://www.childrenoffire.org/index2.asp?include=tissue expand.htm&catID=4.

Van Niekerk, Ashley, et al. "Area Characteristics and Determinants of Hospitalised Childhood Burn Injury: A Study in the City of Cape Town." *Public Health* (2006) 115–24.

———. "Caregiver Experiences, Contextualizations and Understandings of the Burn Injury to Their Child: Accounts from Low-income Settings in South Africa." *Child: care, health and development* 33.3 (2007) 236–45.

Whitman, Walt. "Whitman's Manuscript Drafts of 'Song of Myself,' *Leaves of Grass, 1855.*" http://bailiwick.lib.uiowa.edu/whitman/1855.html.

World Health Organization. "World Report on Child Injury Prevention." http://www.who.int/violence_injury_prevention/child/injury/world_report/Burns.pdf.

CPSIA information can be obtained
at www.ICGtesting.com
Printed in the USA
LVHW08*0526041018
592368LV00016B/71/P

9 781532 647888